The Gate

By
David Wilde

Table of Contents

THE GATE

belongs to GOD

From the first to the last, God opens and closes the gates of life. God is in charge.

It started one morning, at 3 am, with God's voice. He said, *"The Gate."* My reply was, *"What gate?"* That day the journey began; taking me months to understand where God was taking me.

As I was travelling overseas, taking pictures of gates, I asked myself, *"Why?"* God's voice said, *"I want you to write a book."* So the gate is only possible because of God, and from God.

When we read *John 12:49, For I have not spoken, on my own authority, but the Father who sent me has himself given me a commandment, what to say and what to speak, v50 and I know, that his commandment brings eternal life. What I say therefore, I say as the Father has told me.*

So I feel that God has given me a commandment to write the book.

So, all the glory, all the praise, and all the thanks go to God, for He is the Creator.

Through prayer times and my walk and talks with God, Son and Holy Spirit, the pictures and words He gave me, bring us to The Gate.

The Gate

Open your gate and let the King of Glory in…

This book is to encourage readers to walk with God, to listen to His voice and talk to Him. Let God open the gates to your life.

There are many who will try and shut your gates. I encourage you to stay strong in the Lord. He will teach you all you need and more. God will not take you anywhere do anything that Jesus has not already done when He walked this earth. The pain is nothing like the pain Jesus went through for us all.

It was early one morning, about 3 am, when God awakened me from my sleep. God's voice said, *"THE GATE"*. It puzzled me; it seemed to be locked into my mind. When I shared it with others, they said that God was telling me to look after the east gate. There was a new town being built down the road and they thought God was saying to look after the east gate.

But in my spirit, this did not feel right. The next day, I read about the east gate in God's Word. It was not long after that, **that my wife and I** would travel overseas to visit our extended families in England. As we travelled, I took pictures of gates everywhere we went. I said to God, *"Why am I taking pictures of gates?"* God revealed His plan to me. He told me that He would like me to write a book called THE GATE.

I said, "I think you will have to get someone else, as I am not educated enough". God said, "I will help you". So, as I write, God is giving me the words to write. This book is not my book, but GOD'S. So all the glory goes to God, for He is the Way, the Truth, and the Life.

When we go through a gate, it takes us to a destination. It may be a home, a field, or over a bridge. It may be opened or closed. It could be old, rusty or new, big, small, weak or strong. It may be made of wood or steel or concrete. Perhaps it is locked to keep us in that place. Maybe it is a crossing gate to protect us, a fellowship gate, a prayer gate, a love gate, an obedience gate, an encouragement gate, an eye or ear gate. It could be the life gate, the growth gate, the work gate, the marriage gate. There are many, many gates. Do we all have the same number of gates? Or do some have more and some fewer?

Gate One

In November of 1941, the first gate was being opened. A seed was being planted by God, between one man and one woman.

It was during World War II and times were hard. There were bombs everywhere, food was rationed, and many were losing their homes, and even their lives. But God was in control.

The man and woman were being blessed; a new human being was being formed. They were to become my earthly dad and mam. They knew there was a God and 'number three' was on the way. It did not seem like good timing, but God was in charge.

They would pray and go to church down the street, but they couldn't know what God would have in store for their third child. I do not know if God had given them the child's name, but I would say that God had a lot to do with his name. It was to be 'David', meaning 'Beloved' from the Hebrew Dawid probably derived from Hebrew (dwd).

King David was the second and greatest king of Israel, ruling in the 10th century BC. I do not think that the child's earthly dad and mam would have put their young child in the same class as King David, but God was holding this tiny life in His hands and God is the Gate keeper.

God had opened the first gate by planting the seed; the seed of *new life*. This became the first gate of many, as I, that young child, David, take a look back through these gates that God has taken me through.

Gate Two

As this new life had been growing for nine months, the time was drawing near for the second gate to be opened. It was all in God's timing. The day drew closer. God had created a new being; a boy.

Would he be a new messenger that God would mold over his life, and how many gates would be opened to him in his lifetime? His earthly guardians would love and look after him for many years.

The day had arrived for God to open the gate. God's timing was 7th July, 1942. The war was still going strong, food was running low, the bombs were still coming, and people were dying, but life went on. New life, new breath; where would the new gate take him? What was in store for this new baby?

Only God knows the paths we will take.

So, God had blessed two people with great joy; a son had been given to them. He would be the third of five children.

We read in Ecclesiastes 3:1-13 that there is a time for everything, that everything that happens in this world happens at the time God chooses. God sets the time for birth and the time for death.

Gate Three

God starts His work through parents; through their teaching, through their blessings, and through their loving. God opens the gate to the life we live and the paths we will go down. From the first gate, our journeys begin. The track is set, from the planting of the child, to their return to the heavens.

The loud whistles of the bombs, the explosions, and the nights in the shelters, the people praying that the bombs would miss their homes; the war went on and God would keep them safe. The path was not easy; the way would be hard.

The parents would take their children to church and teach them about God; to trust Him and walk with Him. They would read the Bible to them; the stories and the truth that Jesus is the Way, the Truth, and the Light and that God is the One True God.

They did not know what was behind the gate and what gifts God had given the young child, or what talents were in store for him. Would he walk with God and hear God's voice?

Only God knows your path. We look at the trees and see them rising to the heavens. We can walk tall and look good, but only God knows what is inside. He sees every step we take through the gates. When we cut a tree down, we see the growth rings, the beauty of the grain, and the colour. It may only be a small seed, but it can grow to a very large tree. We are small, but with God we can be large.

Would this new life, that God had given this young child's parents, grow as God wanted? Would it be like a very large tree, as the tree puts its roots down into the earth, to get food and to be strong?

Would the child put his roots down into the Word of God, would he get the food out of God's Word? How tall would he grow from God's Word? No one knew, only God.

God created all things. Genesis 1 tells us that in the beginning God created the heavens and the earth. God created all things for man and woman, before He created us. He created us in His image; He put His Spirit and His creativity into us. We are linked into God's will, from the planting of the seed. Will we walk with Him, or away from Him?

Gate Four

Growing and learning about the gifts God has given us; seeing, hearing, smelling, tasting and touching. We start to see and recognize things. This is a gate that we all go through. Our parents are our earthly mother and father. They are the ones that God, our Heavenly Father, has put in charge of the children.

We start to hear their sounds; some we would have heard when we were in the first gate. We hear their voices, our own cries and heartbeat, the voices of young ones around us, and then, the noises of the world and everyday life.

Feeling the pain of being moved, washed and clothed; we start to recognize the smells of the ones looking after us, their touches, and the love they have for us. The love that comes from God, for God is Love.

From the encouragement that they bestow on us, to the gifts and talents that God has created in us, to our health and strength; the path we will walk and the gates we will go through are not known. How many gates will there be? Each day could be a new gate, as each minute we are growing older and learning many things; moving, standing, talking, listening.

Learning to listen is the most important gate we will go through. God has given us ears, but it can take us a very long time to learn to hear God's voice. If and when we go through the wrong gate and walk the wrong path, it may be years before we are put back on the right path by God.

God is with the caregivers; the ones He plants the seeds into, the ones He puts in charge of us, to help us, to teach us and guide us. While we are in this gate, we cannot manage to do anything for ourselves. The caregivers work hard to keep the children clean, guiding us to do the right thing through our working lives.

'Through God all things are possible', psalm 29:1-11. We read this in the Bible, which is the main book to read, as we learn how to listen to God. His plan for us was set when He planted our seed and He made it grow. We can plant seeds, but it is God who makes them grow.

Gate Five

We could call this gate the health gate. God gives us our health and strength. He puts changes, or bends in our paths. Some call these trials, or we could say that He shuts the gate; to bring us closer to Himself. He does not do this to hurt us, but to show us His power and love.

When God's people, the Israelites, were in Egypt, God was there and He was testing them, to see if they were going to be obedient and honour Him. God said that He would go before them. God was opening a gate for the Israelites to a new life and health, and closing the gate to the Egyptians. This became the *death* gate for the Egyptians.

It was at the age of 5 years old that the young child was hit with illness. Was God opening the death gate? The doctors would say that it was 'touch and go'.

In Job 38:17, the Lord challenges Job, "Have the gates of death been opened for you?"

So it was time to seek God and pray for the young child's healing. Would God call him home at this young age? Would the church congregation and others pray for his healing as well?

In the book of Samuel, we read that Hannah was childless. In 1 Samuel 1:9 Hannah said, "If You, God, give me a son, I promise to dedicate him to You." The story goes on to tell us that she did have a son. His name was Samuel and Hannah took him to the Lord's house, to Eli, the priest; where he stayed and learned to walk and talk to God.

Was this the way that the parents of the young child prayed? Did they pray that God would open a new gate, so that the young boy would live? Would he be called to be a messenger, as Samuel was, to walk and talk with God?

13

Samuel had had to learn to hear God's voice. 1 Samuel 3:10, "Speak, Lord, Your servant is listening". Are you listening, or waiting to hear God speak? Is there an Eli at your gate, to help you to hear God?

Would there be an Eli for the young child, or would God, Himself, be the teacher?

When we plant seeds in the ground, we look forward to the seeds growing and producing the flowers or trees or whatever was in the seed packet. But when God plants the seeds, He knows exactly what the seeds will produce and how they will grow. He will weed them, water them, and cultivate them; into what and how He would want them to grow. God will even talk to the seeds.

God will open and shut the gates as the seeds grow and this is all in God's timing. We, as the seeds, do not know we are in each gate, or where the path will lead us. He waits for us to say, "Here we are, Lord, use us?"

Proverbs 1:33 says, "Whoever listens to Me will have security, he will be safe with no reason to be afraid." It also tells us in Proverbs about sitting at the gates. We need to sit at the gate of God, seek Him and then He will guide us by His Spirit, and His Spirit will move us to the right gate.

Gate Six

As the young child grew, worldly things started to pull him through the wrong gates.

In the book of Luke 8, in the parable of the sower; Y'SHUA, (Jesus) was telling His disciples that some of the seeds would fall among thorn bushes which would choke them. So, it's important to keep in the Word of God, as it carries the knowledge to the secrets of the Kingdom of God.

Luke 8:14-15 "The seeds that fell among the thorn bushes stand for those who hear; but the worries and riches and pleasures of this life crowd in and choke them, and their fruit never ripens. Let us hear the message and retain it in a good and obedient heart and persist until we bear fruit."

Verse 15 takes us through other gates. Will the paths be easy and straight? Will it be long before we go through the gate of bearing fruit?

God had heard the prayers of the people and had started to heal the young child. Where would God take him? How many gates would there be in his life? What plans did God have for this young child? Would the seed, that God had planted in him, be fruitful? We can see that God had opened the healing gate.

Hebrews 6:7-8 "God blesses the soil which drinks in the rain that often falls on it, and which grows plants that are useful to those for whom it is cultivated. But if it grows thorns and weeds, it is worth nothing, it is in danger of being cursed by God and will be destroyed by fire."

So, we are the seeds of God, planted here on earth, to follow Him, and to walk and talk with him.

In Jeremiah 29:11-13 We read, "For I AM (GOD) knows the thoughts, plans, and intentions that I AM thinking towards you," says the Lord. "Thoughts of peace and not of evil, to give you a future and hope. Then you will call upon Me and you will go and pray to Me and I will heed you. And you will seek Me and find Me. When you will search for Me with all your heart."

This is just one of God's promises to us all.

2 Chronicles 7:14 gives us another promise. "If we seek Him, with all our heart, then He will be with us. If we humble ourselves and pray and seek His face and turn from our wicked ways, then I (God) shall hear from heaven and forgive their sin and will heal our land and us."

The parents would have to be patient, as it would be weeks before the young child came home. They would give thanks to God for his return to them, continue to teach the boy, as God was teaching them, in the gifts of the Spirit that God has for us all.

This is another gate that God takes us through, as God cultivates our lives into His plans for us and how we can help build His Kingdom. And as we pray, "May His will be done here on earth, as it is in heaven and His will be done in our lives". For His ways are not our ways.

The question was, had the parents of the child made a covenant with God? Had God given them rules to follow and to teach the young child? Had God let them into His plans for the child?

In the Bible, it tells us that God said that the first male child was His. Exodus 13:11-16.

Was this a new covenant, where God was going to bless the second son more than the firstborn son? Had God told them that He would teach the young child to listen to His voice and walk with Him?

Gate Seven

We have come through the *healing* gate. What would God have in store for the young child as he grew older? And as he enjoyed being with God's people and learning more of God and Jesus, through the words read and spoken to him, from the Word of God, the Bible? I think that, at this stage in his life, the Holy Spirit was not a big part of the church life.

Even today, the Holy Spirit is left out and not many people seem to want to know Him. But, when God plants the seeds, He plants Himself, Y'SHUA, and the Holy Spirit in us; the Trinity.

We are all connected together, right from the planting of the seeds. But it's not until we give our hearts to Jesus that God starts to move His plan into action. There will be many, many more gates to go through, as God opens them and shuts them.

The young child had now reached the time to start school; to learn to write and read, and communicate with others.

Y'SHUA, learnt from His father. He sat with the priests and scribes in the temple. He read the Torah, (the first five books of the Old Testament) in the scrolls of that time. But He would always find time to spend with His Heavenly Father, praying and talking together.

As we grow older, we must spend time with God in His Word, walking with Him. We need not be afraid to keep in time with Him, in rhythm, like musicians in a band. If they do not keep the same beat, the sound is not good and they need to start again.

It's the same with God; if we get out of His rhythm, God brings us back on the right paths, to go through the right gates, as we start to use the gifts and talents God has placed in us. Has God got a long list that He ticks off as He goes through them? When God creates a new seed with gifts and talents, health and strengths, and a map of the gates He will take us through, are they mapped out with times between gates?

There are two gates that I believe we have a choice between the gate of blessings or the gate of curses. The better choice for all of us and, one of the most important gates, is the gate to the blessings of God.

The young child had grown taller; would he stay strong and not bend to the things of the world? Would he take the wrong path as he grew into adult life, or would he do the right thing, and choose the gate of blessings?

He had been brought up well, to know right from wrong. Would he have the strength to go up to the mountaintops and down to the valleys? Would he rise up for God, or would he be far away from Him? Would God be his anchor and how long was the rope? How far would he go from God and would the anchor hold him?

The Bible tells us that God's voice is so powerful and so majestic that the voice of the Lord will give strength to his people. (Psalm 29).

Gate Eight

The young child was now older and into worldly things. God had given the child more rope, and the world was opening new gates, the wrong gates. How far would he get down the wrong path? Had he gone through the sin gate?

King David went through the sin gate with Bathsheba. (see ll samuel chapters 11 and 12). The prophet, Nathan, spoke to him so King David went to God with a prayer for forgiveness.

Psalm 51:4-11 "I have sinned, against you and done what You consider evil. Close Your eyes to my sins and wipe out all my evil. Create a pure heart in me, O God, and put a new and loyal spirit in me, do not banish me from Your presence: do not take Your Holy Spirit away from me."

We see that even kings fall away from God, but God is still the Anchor. He gives us enough rope to exercise freedom of choice but we are always in His loving care. We read that David had the Holy Spirit in him, and that He was so precious to him that he did not want God to take His Spirit from him.

Genesis 1:2 says "… and the Spirit of God hovered over the face of the waters." It is so important to keep God's Spirit in us.

The child's caregivers had been teaching him how to live right. They had been guiding him in what was right and wrong, and to help others. God had been developing the talents He had placed in him, as a young child.

What would this next gate be, in the young child's life? What would be in store for him, through this gate? Would God move him in the gifts that He had placed in the young child's hands, as he learned to follow instructions from his teachers, on how to work with wood and other things?

The young child would now start to help others; to draw and cut wood, to make joints to fit the pieces of wood together. He would do the right thing and get along with others, and be happy and joyful in life.

He had started to learn how to be obedient.

In Proverbs 21:3 God says, "to do acts of loving kindness and justice is more acceptable to the Lord than sacrifice."

So, would God teach him obedience, to follow rules and laws, and learn how to be His servant?

Gate Nine

It was time for the young man to start full-time work.

This is another gate that we all go through.

Would he be strong enough, and would he be obedient to keep the laws of the world, whilst also obeying the Lord, his God? This would be an important time for the young man; like any young plant, it would need tender loving care.

God is always there, looking after us, watching, and putting a covering over us. He whispers to us when we go wrong. At the age of 14, it's hard to understand and know God's voice.

Just like Samuel, the young man would have to learn where God was leading him, to find that right job. It was time to help his parents, with the wages he could earn. At this time in his life, the young man was still not sure what gifts and talents God had put in him. He loved working with his hands and building things with wood.

Was God opening this gate, as the young man looked for an apprenticeship in building? He would move from one job to another, making children's toys, hoping for an apprenticeship, but it did not work out. Was God closing this gate?

How do we know when God is leading us? One way is that God is always teaching us. When we look at Moses, in the book of Exodus, at his birth and life in Egypt; God had planted Moses' seed, for His purpose, for His people. Moses' teaching would be used for God's people in his later years. In his youth, Moses would not have had any idea what God had in mind for his life.

The burning bush, where God would speak to Moses, was where God would open the next gate in his life. God told Moses to go back to Egypt, to bring His people out of Egypt and slavery. Moses had run away from that place and could have been at the death gate on his return, (as pharoah wanted moses' death for killing an Egyptian-Exodus 2:15), but God said, "I Am"(a name God called Himself), "will be with you" This had been God's plan right from the planting of Moses' seed. He would walk and talk with God for the rest of his life.

Is God speaking to you? Are you walking and talking with God? Are you on the right path, going through the right gates? God is calling you, God says, "Come to Me." Are you walking in the Spirit of God?

With the disappointment of his last job, the young man moved to another job. He was still young and he still had a lot to learn. Where would this gate take him? Was he still on the right path that God had appointed for him?

Working with older men, fellowshipping with them, and enjoying the work, God was still looking out for him. As he started to explore new places and people, and fellowship with young people his own age, he also began to travel.

The war was long over and the nation was starting to rebuild itself. Temptations of the world were becoming stronger, even though he had been taught right from wrong.

John 15:19 If you were of the world, the world would love you as its own, but because you are not of the world, and I chose you from the world, the world hates you because of this.

The young man had not lost his way, but he was not walking with God. However, God was always talking to him in that very quiet whisper, as if God was sitting on his shoulder. The young man moved into another department at his work place and began learning other skills.

Travelling on holiday, God opened another gate for the young man. Through this gate, his interests turned to a female friend. Had God been moving him from job to job to take him travelling to other countries? Was this all part of God's plan?

Gate Ten

The young man would not find a female friend from his home town. Had God already found the perfect mate for him? His holiday took him to Spain and, whilst there, he met up with four girls but which one had God placed there?

A few days went by and one stood out for him. She was from another town, about 127 miles from his home. On his return home, he would write to her frequently. Was God opening a new gate?

Did God talk to her as well? Was this to be a long term partner for him, to encourage him? Was this part of God's plan for him? Was this God's chosen path for him? Only God knew.

Was this young man ready to take a wife? After months of knowing this girl, it would be time to ask her father for her hand in marriage. Would he say yes? Would this be God's choice for him?

In God's Word, it says that when God brings two people together, they become as one and that when God joins a man and a woman nothing should part them. Matthew 19:4-7

Well, the marriage took place and was a wonderful time. Not only were a man and a woman coming together but two families were aswell. This would be a time for the young newly-weds to work together and get to know each other. As the wife was younger, it was up to the man to care for her. Would God care for both of them? Was this part of God's plan for these two young people?

Months went by. God started to whisper to the young man and, whilst reading the newspaper, he would see an article about workers who wanted to go and work overseas.

We read in the book of Genesis 12:1 that God spoke to Abram; telling him to leave his native land and relatives and go to a country that He would show him.

God said that He would give Abram many descendants that would become a great nation.

Was God behind this quiet whisper? Was God going to open a bigger gate, a new life for the young people?

God was with Abram and told him He would bless him through the seed He would give him. Abram was 75 years old and childless when God made this promise. It would be another 25 years before Isaac was born. Genesis 21: Abram was 100 years and Sarah was 99 years old and God had planted the seed.

Was God calling them to go overseas? If it was God, would He have His way with the young people? They started to look into and apply for the overseas work. Would this be the right move, as they had only been wed for 6 months?

It was to be a big move, leaving all their family behind and moving thousands of miles away. They would not know anyone in this new country. The only things they knew about this place, was what they had learned at school. This was going to be an unknown gate that God would take them through, just like Abraham and Sarah.

In Genesis 17:5-16 God changes Avram and Sarai's names to Abraham and Sarah.

Two months later, the young couple would be on a boat, heading for this new land and life. The journey would take weeks, travelling thousands of miles across oceans, seeing many countries, and meeting many new people along the way. This would be a time for the young people to encourage and support each other. They would feel alone; not knowing that God was in the background, moving them and helping them to learn new things in life.

Days would go by without seeing land, but they would enjoy this time together. They would make new friends who were also moving to this new land to make a new life. Was God with them? The young people could not know, they could not say that God was with them. God had not spoken to the young people then, like He had spoken to Abraham.

Each hour would bring the cargo ship closer to the new country. After being on board the ship for four weeks, this would be an exciting time. Across the seas, the land of New Zealand was getting closer.

Months earlier, in the interview for the job, the city that had been arranged for them was to be Christchurch, in the South Island. But the young people would land in Auckland in the North Island. Was it God that had changed this plan?

They would arrive in the winter, wet and cold and lost. On their arrival they would be moved to a working men's hostel, by bus. on arrival. The manager would tell them that there were no married quarters. Girls were to go one way and boys another way. The young man would stand his ground. **NO**, they would not be split up! They were to be placed at the end of the girls' dorm.

The young people's paper work had been lost. The immigration officer would not be able to find out where the young couple were to go. They would be told to come back the next day, but it would be no better. It would be very disappointing for the young couple to have to go back to the working men's hostel for another night.

By the third day of having no papers, it would be time for the young couple to make a stand. Pledging with the officer, the young man would ask if there was any work in Auckland, with a house. Even though the young couple were not walking with God during this time, was God with them? Was this to be a part of His Plan for their lives?

This would be a time for the young man to be strong and determined; to get a job and a house for his wife, a place they could call home. The officer would return with the name of a place wanting workers with two houses available. The young man would say that he would take the job but...

NO, the officer would tell him that he would have to apply for the job. Once again, they would be very disappointed. Was God testing them to see how determined and strong they were?

Many of the biblical characters were tested so that God could see whether they were true to Him.

What part would the young couple play in God's plan? After tests and interviews they would not be lost, but would find themselves in new work and a new home. God was opening a new gate. The young couple would start to meet new friends and work mates, but after a few months

25

the young man would be thinking that there must be something better for him to do, or was God whispering again? Was God's Spirit, the Holy Spirit, blowing the young man into His plan for him? What was God's plan for him?

God has said that He will never leave us or forsake us. He is always there behind us, before us, and at our side, gently moving us to the place that He wants us to be at a particular time. In His plan for us, God is teaching us to keep in time with His plan. God teaches us how to listen and know His voice; it's like when we started to walk, step-by-step. If we tried to go fast we would fall. God slows us down and if we fall, God picks us up.

When God plants the seed, He never, ever, gives up on it. He provides all we need and teaches us how to walk and talk with Him. From the planting of the seed, we are linked to God, Jesus and the Holy Spirit.

Over the years, the young man had been using his hands to build things; a gift that God had given him. It was now time to move and leave old work friends behind; a new job, building, was to be part of God's plan.

The young wife was now getting homesick for the land she had left and the parents that loved her. Was it time to take her back? Was this in God's plan for them? Was God opening another new gate?

No, God had brought them to New Zealand through His plan and He was not going to let them go back. It wasn't long before the young man would build them a home of their own. God had blessed him with the gifts and talents and good health to do this.

Yes, God was working His plan; moving them into their new home. God had provided.

Ecclesiastes 3b: the time for Building.

Gate Eleven

A new home, a new gate. It would be a time of joy with most of the hard work completed.

Ecclesiastes 3:1-9 talks about the time for planting and refers to the time for making love. The book of Ecclesiastes contains the thoughts of the "Philosopher" who could not understand the ways of God (who controls human destiny). He advised people to work hard, and to enjoy the gifts of God. He also says that the Bible offers hope in God which gives life greater meaning.

The young wife was now settling in to her new home and country. God was providing them with work and providing for all their needs. At this time the husband was working three jobs. One of these jobs was playing drums in a dance band with a young man that the couple had met, only weeks after arriving in New Zealand.

Looking back, you can see that God was working, setting people in place to help the young couple. They would form a wonderful bond with this young man and his wife and their parents. Was this a big part of God's plan?

These new friends would play a big part in their lives. The female friend would become like a sister to the young wife. She did not have any natural sisters. The male friend would become like a brother to the young man as he had left two brothers behind him when they left England. How far ahead was God looking?

Has God got all things written down? He has all things under control. We know that God is the Alpha and the Omega, the Beginning and the End.

As the young couple were working hard, but still not walking with God; where would God take them? They would start a garden, planting fruit trees and vegetables, so they would have fresh food to eat. God was still at work in the young couple, and little did they know that He was about to plant a new seed.

This was going to be a new adventure. God was going to bless them with a child and this would be confirmed by a doctor, but not the gender of the child. What was God going to surprise them with, a boy or girl? Well, it would take nine months to find out.

The young couple were happy, and said that as long as the child was healthy, it didn't matter if it was a girl or a boy. They would accept what God was giving them. Was God's plan coming together?

Also, the other young couple, were in for the same new adventure! God had blessed them as well, and planted a new seed. What different paths would God take them down? Would they continue being very good friends?

They all knew that there was a God, but they did not follow Him. They knew about Jesus, but did not walk with Him.

This was to be a time to put their musical instruments in storage; they needed to devote their weekends to preparing for the children that God was blessing them with, rather than playing in their dance band.

It is true that there is a time for everything, just as it says in *Ecclesiastes 3; there is a time for birth*. God does have all things planned and we are God's creation. We think of a new-born child, so wonderfully made, by the wonderful God that he is. How great He is at putting us together for His plan and works on earth. We do not know how God will guide us, right from the planting of the seed, all through life. We do not know the gates that God will take us through. So we must live life each day for God, with the Trinity; Father, Son and Holy Spirit.

How long would it be before God would speak to the young couple? What was God's plan? God had brought them to New Zealand, but what for? When would God reveal His plan to David, the young man? Would he walk in God's power? Had God heard the cries of His people, like He had heard the cries of the Israelites in Egypt?

Moses had said to God, "I am nobody, so how can I go to Pharaoh and bring the Israelites out of Egypt?" Exodus 3: 11

Would the young man say the same thing to God?

Gate Twelve

Well, the day had arrived and the new seeds were born. A girl had been given to each of the two young couples. What a blessing and a joy for them all. This would be new learning for them, these new children needed us to love, teach, care for and protect them.

We know that God protects us, but He needs us to play our part in a child's life. What a great responsibility God gives to us. Now we must have faith in God, to guide us and teach us to do the right thing. This is all in God's plan and God's blessings for all of His people.

We are all created by Him and so the young couple (now parents for the first time), needed to nurture their baby daughter and spend time with her as she grew.

You might be thinking BUT WHAT ABOUT GOD? Yes, God had been with them from the time He planted their seeds. Wasn't it about time they walked with Him; time to give their life to Jesus?

He has everything good in its time. Also he set the world in their heart, so that no man can find out the work that God makes from the beginning to the end. Ecclesiastes,3:11

Yes, in His time God has every gate, season and time planned.

The young couple decided to return to England for a two year working holiday.

However, it was only to last one year as there was ill-feelings from some members of the families. Was this part of God's plan? I do not think so, but God was protecting them from any hurts and He wanted them back in New Zealand. His plan would be for them there.

It would be another few years before God started to move in their lives. It was now time for their daughter to start school. The couple wanted her to go to Sunday school, at the local church in the town that

29

they had now been living in for some years. Now, what was God's plan? Would it be to use their young daughter in some way in their lives?

One Sunday they had been late picking her up. She decided to walk home. So, when the parents finally arrived, she wasn't there and no one had seen her leave. This would not be a good time for the parents, but on returning, there she was sitting, on the door-step crying.

Was this in God's plan? Now that the worrying time was over, the young girl told her parents that she would not go back to Sunday school, unless they went with her to church. GOD'S PLAN! God has planned every step we take.

So it was to be that the parents would start going to church. Another gate was about to be opened. The mother started to teach in the Sunday school and the father sat in church.

A short time later, the father would be called on to do some repairs to the manse, where the vicar lived. So, God had placed him there, to use the gifts He had given him. The father would continue to go to church on Sundays, and sit at the back, while his young wife started to fellowship with other young wives in the church. There would also be times that the husbands and wives got together to fellowship.

It came to a time within the church when they would have a 'Life in the Spirit' seminar. They were asked to attend and even though they were unsure about it, they had decided to attend. This was to be an eight-week course.

Was God starting to move them? This was to be all new teaching for them and they had just been coming to grips with going to church. A very nice lady in the church would offer to look after their children. By this time, the couple had their little girl and a boy.

She was to take care of them on the nights that the seminar was held. This had helped the young couple to fellowship and pray with others. God was blessing them each day and it wasn't long before God was to plant another seed in the young couple. This seed would be another boy.

Gate Thirteen

It was a short time later that God would start to move in the young man's life. One Sunday morning, they all arrived at the church for the morning service. The wife and children went into the Sunday school block and the male into the church. He sat in the same seat each week; the back row and the seat closest to the door, (this was for a quick get-way) but this morning God would have other plans for him. He still wasn't walking or talking with God.

Something would happen that morning that does not happen to many people. God touched the young man on the shoulder. Who was that? The young man looked around and no one was there. Standing up, he walked around to see if there was anyone hiding near the door, but there was no one. Shaking his head, he went and sat back down.

The music team was just starting to play a song, quietly. The soft music was nice, but then something else happened. The young man was tapped on the shoulder. God spoke to the young man, saying *"I want you up there at the front with them."* The young man said, *"Me?"* God said, *"Yes."* it was clear to the young man that God meant he was to play drums with the music team.

We read in the bible of many instances where God spoke with people; Abram, Jacob, Moses and Saul (who God renamed Paul).

What plans would God have for this young man? The young man was obedient to God and approached the worship leader, who replied "I will have to ask the vicar on this". The vicar told the worship leader to give the young man a trial at their music practice for the next Sunday service. So, the young man went into the loft, to retrieve the drums stored there.

It would not only be the drums that were being retrieved. God was also retrieving the young man, by moving him to where He wanted him to be. The young man would now have to learn how to pray, sing, and

31

worship. This was a new gate for him and God was teaching him how to walk with Him and to listen to His whisper. This would be the path that would take the young man closer to God Himself.

God is so gentle when He places us on His path and works out His plan for our lives.

The young man had been working on a home in his hometown, finishing the job he had started. On this particular day, the owners of the home were out and he was working on a plank between two step ladders when the young man thought he saw someone down the hall. He stopped to look, but found nothing.

A short time later, the same thing happened, so the young man sat and waited and, after a while, two children peeped around the corner of the hall. He had been singing and praising God. The children, who were dressed in clothes from the 16th century or earlier, were now standing right in front of the young man, and asked him who he was singing to. The man replied that he was singing to his God in heaven; worshiping and praising the One True God.

The children asked the young man if they could also sing to God, and he asked them where they were from. They told him that they didn't have a home, but would like to know more about his God. As he began to ask God, in prayer, to accept the children, he heard the Holy Spirit say STOP. He was told that they were spirits of Satan and that they were not welcome in the kingdom of heaven.

Was God giving the young man the gift of discernment? Would this be the beginning of the pictures God would show him?

Were these children the faces of the lost that the Bible tells us about; the souls that are lost in darkness? In Jude 17 there is a warning and an exhortation, to pray in the power of the Holy Spirit.

Behind the scenes, God was working on the young man; moving him to read His Word. He had known his earthly father all his life, but now he had not only met a greater Father, in heaven, but he had a new brother, in Jesus, and the Holy Spirit.

As a very young baby, he had been confirmed. This was the way things had been done when he was born. But the young man had not yet been baptised in the Spirit. A short while later, the vicar invited him to join a team going to minister to another Anglican church in Auckland, at a renewal weekend. He was asked to play the drums, with some of the others in the team. He was learning to walk with God. He was interested in what God might do for other church members? The young man was just learning how to pray with others.

Saturday was a long day and was now over and the group was leaving early Sunday morning. Afterwards, having finished lunch with his wife and children, and as the young wife was heading home with the children; she told him that she would be back with more of the group for the night meeting. The young man was glad about that. While sitting on a park-type bench alone, with not many people around, a strange thing started to happen.

Four or five sparrows flew down to him and one sparrow perched on the back of the bench, about two feet away from where he sat. Another was on the ground in front of him, about the same distance away. The rest of the sparrows were spread out around him. Hoping no one could hear him, the young man started to speak to them.

"Sorry, I have no food for you." As he said this, they all flew off, but only minutes later, there were about a dozen around him. Forming a similar pattern, with one on the back of the bench and the rest chirping away; it was as if this bird was telling him something, or telling the others everything was okay, as some had drawn even closer than before.

The young man started to talk to them again, saying, "I see you have brought some of your friends with you this time, but I still have no0 food for you." Again, they flew away, but minutes later they were back once again with more of their friends. Resting in the same pattern as before, he was certain that it was the same bird that perched in the same place, on the back of the bench, every time.

This little sparrow had to be either chirping to the young male or to his other thirty or more friends, but why? With the sparrows still gathered around him, as he was puzzling about what had happened he heard God say: *"Do you see the sparrows? They are like My people. Some will come close to Me, some will stand back and some will stay even further away. They fear me. I want My people closer to Me, like the sparrow that sat on the back of the bench. I want them to speak to Me and not be worried or fear Me."*

33

Matthew 6:26 says that we are worth more than the birds and some versions talk about two sparrows.

That night, as the group met in prayer for the night meeting, this same Scripture verse would be spoken out by one of the group. The young male thought, "Wow! God is in control from morning to night!"

Matthew 6:33 But you must continually seek first the kingdom of God and his righteousness then all these things will be provided for you. V 34 therefore do not be anxious for tomorrow. For tomorrow will be anxious of itself. Each day's trouble is enough for this day.

What was God calling the young man to do? Was God telling him to bring His people near to Him? But he had only just started to go to church. Didn't you have to go to Bible College before you could minister to God's people? Isn't it the job of a vicar or a pastor to lead people to God, to be a shepherd of His sheep?

The man would ponder these questions, wondering what God was really saying to him, as he wandered the streets surrounding the meeting place. Heading back to the church, he watched as others arrived for the meeting and wondered if they too, were asking the same questions: "What was God going to do? Who will God minister to? Will the Holy Spirit move?

That night, God would have another surprise for the young man. The vicar started the meeting with a prayer, a song and more prayers, as the young man played the drums quietly with the other musicians in the background. He sat between the two large concrete columns that held the building up, in the basement of the church, where the meeting was being held. The other musicians, and the two entry doors were to his left. During the prayer time following the worship, while all eyes were closed, he saw, in a vision, the two large doors burst open. Flames of fire surrounded and engulfed him.

Terrified, the young man tried to move closer to his wife and others in the group, but he could not move a muscle. The fire was overpowering him. No one tried to help because no one could see or feel what was happening to him. The entire experience seemed to last about two or three minutes. Was this God baptizing him in the Holy

Spirit? And why? He had not been asking God for His Spirit and he was just a beginner at church life. What was God moving the man into?

God would begin to show the young man more pictures. Was God taking him into the supernatural world, the realm of the Holy Spirit? Was God taking him through another new gate? What was God going to do next in his life? Would God's Holy Spirit begin to convict him about areas of his life that were not pleasing to God?

While the young people and their children were visiting their families in the old country, he met up with an old school pal. His old friend had given his life to the Lord? but was having problems in the church he was attending at the time. They arranged a time to pray together; to come before the Lord their God.

That night, joined by the school friend and his brother-in-law, as they were praying, the young man felt the three of them were to hold hands. God then took him into a vision. As if he was looking on from behind the small group, he saw a very bright glow that he understood to be the presence of God, with three silhouettes holding hands; his friend, his brother-in-law, and himself.

The young man heard God say, *"Who do you have here?"*

"Brian on my left and Alan on my right; they brought a problem to You, God," he replied.

Then God said, *"I'm placing a covering over Brian, to protect him. NO arrows from the powers of darkness will penetrate his being. The covering is like a board that the arrows cannot go through."* How wonderful, just like Moses at the burning bush, we were right in the presence of God!

Gate Fourteen

God would continue to mold the two young people more and more. His plan for them would unfold step-by-step; pulling out the weeds in their lives, helping them to learn and listen to the Spirit of God.

It would not be good for us to know God's plan for us ahead of time. Through the Bible we read that when we walk with God, He is our Buckler. Psalm 25: 1-4 A buckler is like a large shield which covers the front of the body. In a battle, when soldiers got close to a wall, the large shield in front and the small shield above their heads protected them from the arrows. This is how God protects us.

It wasn't long before God would move the young male. He wasn't settled in the Church of England (Anglican). He felt as if he was on a railway station waiting for the right train. Feeling a bit lost one day, he thought that it may be time to go away alone, to seek the Lord in prayer and fasting. Would he meet with God, Jesus or the Holy Spirit? What would God have for him this weekend?

All he would have with him was his Bible, some music tapes and tea to drink. The place he chose was near the beach, nice and quiet. It was a small building at the bottom of a cliff, with the beach right at the front door. He decided that this would be a good place to meet with the Trinity.

He would get settled in for the night, singing and worshipping the Trinity. The old wooden building had a large light fixed to it that lit up the sand on the beach. It was getting late and very quiet as he bowed in prayer before God. The wind began to rise outside and the lamp began to rattle. Then the whole building started to move and shake and he thought it was an earthquake.

"Please don't let big rocks fall from the top of the cliff and crush the building," the fearful young man prayed. Soon he realized that it was Satan trying to stop him from worshipping God, Jesus and the Holy Spirit. As he cried out to God, he sensed Him telling him that he could stop Satan. So he shouted out in a loud voice, "GET AWAY FROM HERE SATAN. YOU ARE NOT WELCOME HERE, IN JESUS' NAME."

Mark 11:24 "For this reason I tell you when you pray and ask for something, believe that you have received it, and you will be given whatever you ask for."

Here he was, standing up, in the name of Jesus, telling Satan to go. Instantly, the noise and the wind STOPPED, you could have heard a pin drop. Afterwards, in the quietness, the young seed received from God the gift of speaking in a different language; the gift of tongues.

Read Acts 2

God was blessing him with all these things. Where would God take him next? Which gate would God open next and what other gifts would God give him? Was it God that whispered to him about going away for the weekend? Was it God that was moving him along the path He had for him?

It wouldn't be long before the two young people and their children moved from the Anglican Church to the Baptist Church. At the time, the local Baptists were a small congregation, meeting in a small building. A new young pastor was preparing to take over from their old pastor, (who was ill). New things were being planned; a bigger building to hold more people. They had purchased a bigger block of land and were in the process of selling the old building.

The male was not only invited to play in the worship team, but was also asked to take part in the building of the new church home. Had God already planned this many years before? During his growing years, had God been equipping him with particular gifts and talents? Was this yet another gate, that God was taking him through?

Before the congregation moved out of their old building, one of the elders came to the two young people and encouraged them both to be water baptised. They were to have been the last people to be baptised in the old building. While the new building was being completed, the congregation moved their meetings to the town hall. This would prove to be a hard time for the male, as he balanced running the work on the new building while still maintaining his own business and workers.

37

Throughout this trial however, God blessed them all abundantly with good health and strength; keeping everyone who worked on the new church building safe.

While God continued to lead them in to a deeper understanding of the gifts of the Spirit, he joined a home group. The group's leader, who was walking in the Spirit, was very encouraging and many times during prayer, God would give him words and pictures. Some-times God would enable him to see the Spirit fall on other members of the group, or see very fine dust-like gold fall on others. This would be something he would often encounter, as he walked with God.

When the young man was asked to share his testimony with the group for the first time, they asked him how he had come to know GOD and how he had been baptised in the Holy Spirit. After telling them his story, the group's leader said, *"WOW!"* Acknowledging that he had been mightily filled with the Holy Spirit, he assured him that there was no one on earth who would be able to put out the fire of the Holy Spirit that burned within him; that he was completely immersed in the Holy Spirit.

Gate Fifteen

God moved him to another new gate in his walk with Him. Through the Spirit, God moved him during the worship time, pointing out people to pray for. He would go to them, lay hands on them and pray. Why was God doing this? Was it because he was obedient? Was he listening to God or was God testing him?

The Bible tells us that God's ways are not our ways. Isaiah 55:8-9 When God speaks, He already knows what is going to happen while we worship Him, Jesus, and the Holy Spirit. In the Word of God, it tells us that when two or three are gathered in His name, there I am in their midst. Matthew 18:20.

While he was visiting a church in England, a man wanted prayer for his friend. During the worship, the Spirit was stirring within the young man, but he was unsure of what God wanted to do through him. At the end of a song, the pastor's wife asked him to come and anoint the man with oil. After also asking others to come, almost the entire congregation moved forward, as he began to pray and anoint this man. The Spirit led him to tell the man that, while he stood in the gap for his friend, he was to pray over him, as the power of God was on him for healing. The Spirit then told the man to anoint everyone and he praised and thanked God for using him. He was learning to listen very carefully to God through His Spirit.

We see that God is always there when we walk with Him, even though we are never sure when or where He will use us. If we were to listen to the wrong voice, Satan's voice, then we would be taken through the wrong gate and on a different path. So, we must learn to know the voice of God.

Matthew 13 :14, and the Prophecy of Isaiah is fulfilled "you hear but you do not understand" and seeing you will not see or understand. When we hear the Shepherd we, His sheep, will follow Him through the right gate. We are to be obedient to what God asks us to do, and to have a good countenance when we do His will.

In Exodus 34: 29-35 we read that Moses had a very good countenance on him, most of the time his face shone, and they were afraid to come near him, when God spoke to him. he had to uncover his face. Exodus 25 and 34 tells us, that God told Moses to build the temple and all that was in it, that He gave Him the Laws, the Ten Commandments. When we read God's Word and take it into our spirits, we are building ourselves up with His commandments and laws, because we are the temple of the Holy Spirit. When it was finished, the cloud covered the temple, and the dazzling light of the Lord's presence filled it. The cloud remained over it through the day and fire during the night (Exodus 40:34-38).

God said, that He would not leave us or forsake us, as if that cloud covers us, for was He not in the cloud? Could the fire at night be the Holy Spirit in us? In Gate Thirteen, the young man was engulfed in the flames of the Spirit. God is working 24/7 to mold us into what He wants us to be. Just as all the things that went into the temple were anointed and sanctified, we read in God's Word, that we too, are anointed and sanctified to be set apart. To be made holy, purified, and made free from sin. Perhaps it is only when we go through the last gate, that we are sanctified.

How long does God keep us in each gate? When we go through a gate, does God lock the gate behind us, so that we cannot go back? The Bible tells us not to look back. How does God get our attention? With Moses, it was through a burning bush that God spoke to him. Moses was to lead the sheep through the gate, but he did not want to go through it himself. He asked God to send someone else. Moses was filled with fear while in the wilderness, listening and speaking to a burning bush, just like the young man was, listening and speaking to the birds. God told Moses that his job was to bring His people out of Egypt. Was God telling the man that his job was to bring His people closer to God Himself?

It was in 2013 that God opened the man's eye gate and helped him to see what He had been saying to him through the birds. God wanted his people closer to Him. This gate had been locked in his heart for over 40 years, for God makes all things come to pass in His time.

You may be asking, (how do we come closer to God)? We come closer to Him through His whisper, through His Word, through prayer and praise, through walking and talking with Him. These are ways we can open our gates to spend time with God, our Creator.

When we come to the Father, we also come to the Son and the Holy Spirit. We can get to know each person of the three-fold trinity, in a wonderful way, no matter where we are or when we find the time to connect.

There are three ways we can learn, three gates:

Seeing.

Hearing

Doing.

When Jesus took the Last Supper, the bread and the wine, they were laid out on the table where His disciples could see them. He said, "Do this to remember Me," so they could hear. As they ate and drank, they were doing. So every day we go through in our walk with God, He teaches us and draws us closer to Himself.

While the couple were on holiday in Vancouver, God woke him at 2 a.m. in the morning. He began praising and giving thanks to God, in his mind for the new day, so as not to waken his wife. He thanked God for all that He was doing in their lives. He dwelt on how big God was and that, as the Bible tells us, we are like a speck of dust or a grain of sand in His hand.

As he lay there in the presence of God, he heard the Spirit say, "People do not comprehend just how big God is. They say that their God is 'so big, so strong, and so mighty, that there's nothing their God cannot do'.

"But, do they trust in Him?" The Spirit went on to say, "Wi-Fi. People have phones or iPads. When they want to communicate with each other, they can go into buildings, homes, or churches that are connected to Wi-Fi, and be plugged in, but they need the password. In the same way, people can connect with God as He has built in them His Wi-Fi. All they need is the password; the Holy Spirit that is also built into them all right from the day He created them. To communicate with God is still easy; bow a knee and pray.

Reading in Genesis 18, the Lord appeared to Abraham, as he was sitting at the entrance of his tent. He looked and saw three men standing there and as soon as he saw them he ran out to meet them, bowing to them with his face to the ground. After feeding and watering them, one of the visitors asked where his wife, Sarah was, and he answered that she was in the tent. "Nine months from now I will return and your wife Sarah will have a son," he said to Abraham.

Sarah laughed when she heard. "Can I really have a son when I am so old?" She did not trust in Him. Abraham went with them and God did not hide from him what he was about to do. Abraham pleads for Sodom. God had made a promise to Abraham. God had chosen him in order that he may command his sons and his descendants to obey God, and do what is right and just.

Abraham would plead for the believers in Sodom and Gomorrah, but their sins were very great. Abraham pleaded five times and God saved only Lot's family; four people. They were told not to look back, but Lot's wife did and she was turned into a pillar of salt.

This story in Genesis teaches us to obey God, to do the right thing, and to stand up against the sins of the world. The Trinity will help us, to be strong and steadfast in our Lord God.

The Great Tribulation
The beginning of woes

Mark 24:3 After he sat down (this is Y'shua) upon the Mount of Olives, The disciples came to him privately saying, "you must now tell us when these things will be," and "what will be the sign of your coming and the end of the age." (Please read 4-27) 27 says, "for the light, comes out from the east, and shines until the west, so will be the coming of the Son of Man:" V 29 But immediately after the affliction of these days, the sun will be darkened, and the moon will not give its light, and the stars will fall from the sky, and the power of the heavens will be shaken. (Isa.13:10, Ezek. 32:7)

How do we fully worship God? I know that Jesus said to worship the Father with all our mind, soul, strength and heart, this is the greatest and first commandment, and the second is to love our neighbour like we love ourselves. Matthew22:37-38

Many times we get pictures of things we do not understand. The man was visiting St George's, a small church in the north east of

England, when the Lord gave him a picture of two pairs of hands belonging to a man and a woman. They were bound with chains and the Spirit told him that they needed to be set free. Without knowing whether they were married or single, he shared this with the congregation, but at the time, no one came forward. Had he got it wrong?

Later that day, he got an email from his sister asking him to pray for Penny, David, and their son about the picture he received on Sunday morning. He prayed for them to be set free, to be healed, and to know God's presence. He trusted that God would work in their lives, as he praised God, for what He was doing in his own life and helping him to pray for others.

When we trust in God, He will do mighty things through us. *In Genesis 28 we read about Jacob running away from his brother. We cannot run away from God. God will shut the next gate. Jacob took a rock to lay his head on to sleep. As Jacob slept, he dreamed of a stairway from earth to heaven and angels going up and down.*

In Psalm 28 David said that God was His rock. Is God your rock? Jacob and David both knew when they were in the presence of the Trinity. When we come into the presence of God, are we sure that we are in His presence? Are we standing on the God, the Rock? Are we rock solid in God?

As he grew older, the man was sensing the presence of God more and more each day. One Sunday night, he went out for a walk with his wife, her sister, brother-in-law and niece when they came to a small church that was having a night service. As they went to enter, he sensed that God wanted to speak with him, and that he was not to go into the service. He walked around the building, speaking to God about how very old the building was.

When he arrived back at the main doors and looked in, he still felt he was not to go in. Sitting on a seat outside the doors, he watched many people go by without looking at the church. When one couple walked past, the woman stopped, as if she would like to go in. The man looked at the church, put his arm around her and turned her away from the building, but as they walked away she looked back.

God told the man that lots of people were lost, sad, sick, angry, and worried, and that most of them did not want to know Him, or even look at His place of worship.

How do we turn people to God? What can we do for the kingdom of God?

Gate Sixteen

It is important that when we walk and talk with God, we keep strong, steadfast, and obedient to His calling. I cannot stress this enough! If you are just starting out, stay close to the Trinity. The powers and spirits of Satan are all around us and he will try and stop us from bringing a message from God.

Many times, when the man would bring a message from God, he would be attacked by someone within the church family. Sometimes he was stopped Satan will use anybody to do his dirty work.

In Gate Thirteen, the man encountered spirits in the two children. It is important to have the gift of discernment, to have the power of the Trinity within you.

In Romans 16:17-19, Paul says, "... and I urge you, brothers, to look out for those who make dissensions and draw you away from the true doctrine contrary to the teaching which you learned, and you must continually turn away from them. For such as these are not serving the Lord our Messiah but their own gluttony. And through smooth talk and flattery they could deceive the hearts of the innocents. For your submission has been heard by all: so I rejoice with you."

One day, the man had to have some stitches to his nose and a few days later, he was talking to God and heard Him say, *"It would be good if My people would stitch themselves to Me."*

The man asked, *"What do you mean?"*

"You see the stitches to your nose," God replied. *"When you have stitches, they close up the wound so that germs can't get in and they help the wound to heal. If My people would be stitched close to Me, then I could heal them."*

Another time, God spoke to the man about being glued to Him. The man could not understand. He thought to himself, *"God is in the heavens and I am on the earth, so how can we be glued together?"*

"No look," said God. *"When you take two pieces of wood, put glue on each piece and clamp them together, they cannot be parted. "That's how I want My people to be with Me, the Lord, their God. Stuck to Me, so that we cannot be parted."*

The word of God says to forgive others. *Luke 11:4. People say things to us which hurt us, they trespass against us. The Lord's Prayer says to forgive those who trespass against us.* We must do this as soon as we can, so that their words do not eat into our hearts and start to take root.

In Proverbs 24:12 it tells us that God looks at our hearts. V 12 if you say, Behold, we did not know it. Does not he who ponders the heart consider it? and he who keeps your soul, does he know it? And will not he render to every man according to his works?

We can do lots of works for God, but if our hearts are not right with Him we labour in vain.

On one occasion the man was listening to music at his sister's home, with his eyes closed He was lifted up in the Spirit and moving among the clouds. Moving closer to the blue sky above him, he looked down on the earth over the roads and fields. It was so peaceful, soaring like an eagle. Although this vision only lasted a few seconds, time seemed to stand still. As he started to descend slowly, he began to see the faces of people. The first face he saw was that of his earthly father who had passed away. Many other faces appeared, of people he had never met. He asked, *"Are they spirits of the kingdom or are they lost spirits?"* Was this another gate?

A few days later he received a text from his prayer partner with three Scripture references: 1 Thessalonians 5:23-24; 2 Peter 1:5-9; and 1 Corinthians 1:1-31. When he was reading the chapter in 1 Corinthians, verses 26-29 spoke to him, and he thought of how very blessed he was to know Jesus as his Lord.

1 Corinthians 1:30 says, "But because of him you are in the Messiah Y'SHUA."

1 Thessalonians 5:24 says, "The One who calls you is faithful, who also will do what He has said."

In 2 Peter 1:8, "For as these things are present and multiply in you, they do not make you useless, or fruitless, in the knowledge of our Lord Y'SHUA Messiah."

46

2 Peter 5-7 talks about moral goodness, faith, knowledge, patience, with self-control, godliness, brotherly love."

These scriptures were so encouraging to the man. When God told him to write this book, he did not think that he was the right person to write it. But God said, "I will help you." So we are so blessed when God leads us through the right gate, and along the right path. Praise God, as He takes us through each gate, AMEN!

One morning, during his prayer time, Father God was telling the man, through the Spirit, about the garland of Jesus. When we visit some pacific islands, on arrival, they place a garland around our necks. The Holy Spirit told him that the garland of Jesus was much bigger and that it covers us completely. We are protected by the Trinity.

"My son, listen! Obey the instruction of your father! Do not forsake the teachings of your mother! V9 for they will be a garland of grace for your head and chains about your neck. Proverbs 1:8-9.

During his prayers he told God that he was still not sure that he could write 'The Gate'; that he was just not educated enough to write a book.

That morning, during his readings, he read that Moses had been told to write down these words for himself, for in accordance with these words I have cut a covenant with you and with Israel. God encouraged the man through the words of *Psalm 17* and he knew that he had to try and be obedient to His call.

That day's readings told the man that, as we are the guards to our doors, so must we be the guards to our gates, and that we must be sure to guard them well, against all that may come against them. We read in Nehemiah where they built the walls and gates with the doors. *Nehemiah 7:3 and I(God) said to them, Do Not let the gates of Jerusalem be opened until the sun is hot.* So we see that the gates were locked to protect them. *Nehemiah 13;20, so the merchants and sellers of all kinds of ware lodged outside Jerusalem once or twice.* So we see that we must guard against all that comes against us.

God asked him, "What would you do if the hinges on your gate were rusty and it was hard to open? "I would oil it to get it working, so it would be free to open," he answered.

If we keep the gate well-oiled and free for the Trinity, are we willing to open it for them to work in our lives? When we open the gate, is the path from the gate short or long, clear or full of trials and hard to walk? Must we guard it from all the cares of this world? *God said to cast all your cares on Him, for He cares for you and loves you.*

As the man would read the word of God, sometimes He would only give him one word. One day, God gave him three words: poor, money, and tongue. He began to think that maybe God was telling him about other gates.

The poor and afflicted gate

When I think of the poor and afflicted, I think of the greed of the world. *Jesus said that we are to look after the poor.*

The money and riches gate

This makes me think of the leaders and governments of countries. They spend money on wars, travel for themselves and put millions into sport. Millions and millions of people worship sport. It has become their god and they have pushed the Lord God away. Jesus did not die for this. He died for our sins and so that we could come closer to His Father, the One that created us all.

The tongue gate

The tongue lets us taste the good food we eat and enjoy, but it can also be the most poisonous part of a human's body. God gave it to us for sharing love and the gospel, but it is like poison when we say the wrong things to people.

Sometimes we will go through the afflicted gate and the tongue gate. When we put God first and speak out His Word, we get closer and closer to the Trinity of the Father, Son, and Spirit.

Psalm 24: 7 says, "Fling wide the gates, open the ancient doors and the Great King will come in." Who is this great King? He is the Lord, strong and mighty.

Proverbs 24:7. talks about the gates. It says, "Wisdom is too high for a fool: he does not open his mouth in the gate.

About two and a half thousand years ago, they would sit at the gates. The gate was a place to do business and to greet people to the city. The gates of the city were an important meeting place. In *Ruth* 4:1 Boaz went to the gate to find Ruth's kinsman and the elders would also sit at the gate in order to be witnesses, and to see that everything was settled justly before God.

We can go to the prayer gate to talk with God and, through the prayer gate we can go through other gates; to give thanks, lift up the sick, our families, and to find out what God would like us to do. It's important to bring all things to God, at our prayer gates and other gates that He takes us through.

"Come then my love; my darling, come with me. You are like a dove that hides in the crevice of a rock. Let me see your lovely face and hear your enchanting voice." - Song of Songs 2:13b-14

Throughout the Bible God is calling us to come, for He loves us so much. We do try to hide from God, but He wants us to come closer. He really wants to see our faces and hear our enchanting voices. He wants us to speak with Him, just as Adam and Eve did in the Garden of Eden. After eating the forbidden fruit, they tried to hide from God. God wanted to fellowship with them, just as He wants to fellowship with us; regularly, daily. Daniel would speak with God three or four times a day and He accomplished much through Daniel. Are you ready to walk with God in the Garden?

Gate Seventeen

In Song of Songs 7:14 we read about mandrakes.

"The mandrakes give off a smell, and at our gates are all manner of pleasant
Hebrew Scriptures Edited and Greek NT Text translated by William J. Morford 2011

G BPC-FV fruits, new and old, which I have laid up for you, O my beloved." – Song of Songs 7:14

"One New Man, Bible. Revealing Jewish roots and power. 2011 by Rev William J Morford" foot note to 7:14 Just what mandrakes were is not known, but the assumption is that this fruit is related to love. From Gen. 30:14 and from the Hebrew Name "dodaim" which is related to "dodim" meaning "love"

I am thinking, that this is the gate of the fruits of the Spirit.

Spiritual Gifts

1 Corinthians 12:1

12: 1, And concerning the spiritual, brothers, I do not want you to be ignorant. V2 - because you know that when you were heathens somehow you were being led away, being led astray to dumb idols. V3. On this account I am making known to you that no one says, speaking in the spirit of God. "Curse Y'shua." and no one is able to say, "Lord Y'shua." except by the Holy Spirit. Please read through V4 – V11.

V11. But the one and the same spirit operates all these things, distributing His own gifts to each, just as He wishes. The Bible tells us that there are nine fruits of the spirit.

1 Corinthians 13:1 tells us what the fruit of the Spirit does for us and the other gates God takes us into. These gates are very important to us as we go through the gate of life. So love is one, and is the key to the gates, and if we do not have love, then we will not go through many gates.

50

"But the fruit of the Spirit is love, joy, peace, patience, kindness, goodness, faithfulness, gentleness, self-control." - Galatians 5:22.

So we must walk closely with the Trinity.

The man remembered back to when God first called him and that he had a very bad temper. Often, if something went wrong when he was working with power tools, he would throw the power tool as far as he could, in his anger, or use very bad language. He knew that this kind of reaction was not a good witness for God. But, through the Holy Spirit, God showed him how much He cared for him. God began a good work in him and removed his anger and bad language. When this happened his workmates began to see the change in him.

One day He was in the garden weeding and as he pulled up weeds God said to him, *"You see the weeds; some have small roots and others have very long roots. As you can see, the small rooted weeds come out very easily, but the weeds with long roots take a lot more pulling. It's the same with your sins; some come out easily and some take longer to get rid of. No matter how many weeds and sin you have in your life, I will never, never give up on you."*

John 3:16; "For God so loved the world, that He gave His only son, so that everyone who believes in Him would not die but have eternal life. V17. For God did not send his Son into the world so that He would condemn the world, but so that the world would be saved through Him.

(James) Jacob 4:13 Come now! Those who say, "Today or tomorrow we will go into this city and we will work there a year and we will carry on business and we will make a profit." V14. Yet you do not understand what your life will be tomorrow: for you are vapor, appearing briefly, then also being made invisible. V15. Instead you ought to say. "If the Lord wills and we will live, then we will do this or that V16. But now you boast in arrogance: all boasting such as this is evil. V17. So then someone who knows that he should do good but does not do it, it is sin for Him. (NOTE the book of James in most Bibles is the book of Jacob in the One New Man Bible. The Greek title of this book is Iakob)

We do not know what God has written in His book for us. When God awakens you from your sleep at 3.15am, do you give thanks and praise to Him and ask Him to continue to be with you? Do you ask God what He wants and listen to what He says?

The man mentioned to a friend once that sometimes he woke through the night and praised God, but that sometimes he fell asleep praying. The friend assured him that, in the presence of the Lord God, this was a good place to fall asleep. In the habit of rising at 6am to pray and read God's word, he would ask God to forgive us, His people, for not doing our part; for not standing up for the right things. Noah stood up for God, praying against the sexual sins of the world.

Noah was a Godly Man.

Genesis 6:5 And God saw that the wickedness of man was great in the earth, and every imagination of the thoughts of his heart was continually only bad. V6. And the Lord was sorry that he had made man on the earth, and it grieved him in his heart. V7. And the Lord said, "I shall destroy man, whom I have created, from the face of the earth: man, beast, the creeping things, and fowls of the air, for I am sorry that I have made them." V8. But Noah found favor in the eyes of the LORD.

Noah was a just man. He had three sons, Shem, Ham, Japheth.

Noah walked with God, God asked Noah to build a Tevah, which means Box.

I think Noah was thinking, that's easy, picturing a small box, then he is given the dimensions: 450 feet by 75 feet by 45 feet – staggering.

V17. And, behold, I AM, even I, am bringing a flood of water upon the earth to destroy all flesh, in which is the breath of life, from under heaven, and everything that is on the earth will die." Noah was in his six hundredth year when called by the Lord, there were only eight people in the box along with all the animals.

The man was thinking about Sodom and Gomorrah. Abraham asked God to have mercy on Sodom and Gomorrah because his nephew Lot and family lived there. *Genesis 13: 8 And Abram said to Lot, "there must be no strife, I pray you lot" between me and you, and between my herdsmen and your herdsmen, for we are brothers." V10 is where Lot moves to the plain of Jordan to Sodom, V 13:12 Abram lived in the land of Canaan, and God gives all the land of Canaan to Abram. V16, is where God says he will make his seed as the dust of the earth.*

Chapter 17:5, this is where Abram gets his name changed to Abraham.

Chapter 17:15 is where Sarai gets her name changed to Sarah

Chapter 19:17 this is where the two angels took Lot, his wife and their two daughters out of the city. The angels said to them "Do Not Look Back." 19 :26 But his wife looked back from behind him and she became a pillar of salt.

2 Peter: 2. False Prophets and Teachers.

V2. Many will then follow in their unbridled lusts, because of which the way of truth will be blasphemed, V3. and they will use you for their gain with made up messages in their greedy desire to have more, for whom the judgment has for a long time not been idle and their destruction is on its way. V4. For if God did not spare angels when they sinned, but, after He held them in pits of darkness in Tartarus, He gave them over, guarding them until judgment. V5. Nor did He spare the ancient world, but when He brought a flood on an ungodly world He guarded Noah, a preacher of righteousness, and seven others. V6. Again with the cities of Sodom and Gomorrah, when He reduced them to ashes in destruction He condemned them as He made them an example for those who were going to be ungodly.

In his time with God from 3.15am God was working on his prayers to Him, God was wanting him to pray this way and He confirmed this through *2 Peter 2:2.* when we read this book of Peter we need to be with God like Noah, Abraham and Lot, and many others in his word, that we are close to God the father, to live his word and not just read it, God created us for a purpose.

What a God we have! He shows us how to pray and never stops teaching us through His Word, even in our sleep. Amen! Never be amazed at what God says to you or the pictures He shows you.

One morning, during a pre-church service prayer time, God, through His Spirit, showed the man a large plate of HOT CHIPS. "WHAT?" he exclaimed. He heard God say, *"All over the world, people know of, and like hot chips. My people in the church family are the 'hot chips' and through Gods word, Jesus's name will be known throughout the world. Jesus tastes better than hot chips!"*

Revelation 3:15- 18.

V15. I know your deeds, that you are neither cold nor hot. I wish you were cold or hot. V16. Because you are lukewarm in this way and neither hot nor cold, I am going to spew you out of my mouth. V17. Because you say "I am rich and I have become wealthy and I do not need anything," but you do not know that you are the wretched and miserable and poor and blind and naked.

Through the man's small group of three, he learnt how important it was to have prayer partners. They would often meet on Wednesday nights at 7pm, to pray and give thanks to God. For two hours they would seek God's leading and the Holy Spirit would take them on a journey in prayer; working through them in intercession, praying for a person, a place, or a building. When the group first started, they had no idea that they would be together for many years. Many times, the man would see visions of horses. Once, as one of them was praying, he saw a picture of a very large, light-blue horse with wings and no rider. It was very majestic. He had been told that horses were symbolic of the power of God Himself, and that when he saw horses, God was showing him that He was there, that His presence was before him.

One morning, during his prayer time, while reading *Jeremiah 6:27-28, the man really felt like God was saying, "I have set you among My people as an assayer and tester, so you can know and try their ways. They are all grievous revolters, walking with slanderers. They are bronze and iron; they are all corrupters."* Had God put him in the Baptist Church, to use him as a tester? Was this why he saw pictures in the Spirit?

When reading about the prophets in the Old Testament, I think that it must have been hard for them to have to take a message to the people. Often I suspect that they would have closed their ears to the messages from their God.

The man was older now so he would have to be obedient to God's voice, when God gave him a message to deliver to the people of the church. He prayed that he would be strong and get stronger in the ways of the Trinity, Amen.

Jesus was always telling His followers to keep praying and listen to what God was saying to them. Praying, reading God's Word and giving thanks for all things are all important keys in our walk with God. The eyes of God are on us all the time. God is so faithful and loving that He is with us 24/7.
"For the eyes of the LORD run to and fro throughout the whole earth, to show Himself strong to those whose heart is loyal to Him..." 2 Chronicles 16: 9 (NKJV)

One Sunday morning during the service, God spoke to him, prompting him to pray against the spirit of domineering that had been coming down from generation to generation. God told him that He wanted it to be stopped and that this spirit was not just using men, but women also. So, he rebuked the spirit of domineering and asked God to cleanse them. God was speaking through him so powerfully and with such authority, that the people would know this was from God Himself.

It is most important to bow the knee before our God, lifting up our hearts to Him and listening to what He is saying. Jeremiah was thrown into a cistern where there was no water, only muddy clay. He sank into the miry clay, but God saved him. Jesus saved us out of the miry clay, he stood our feet on the rock. Jesus is our rock, Amen. When we give our hearts to the Trinity and we start to walk with Them, they hold the rope that pulls us up out of that miry clay, Yes, Jesus died for us upon that cross.

How great it would have been for the disciples to walk and talk with Y'SHUA, to stand next to Him and hear Him teach from the Torah (teachings). It was wonderful then and it's wonderful now that when we pray to God, Jesus and the Holy Spirit, we can come into the presence of the Trinity. As we pray, praise and worship the Trinity more and more, we can begin to feel to sense, and to know that They are right there beside us. Just as it was wonderful for the disciples, it is wonderful for us, as we feel the love of God on us.

2 Chronicles 25:2 tells us that Amaziah did what was pleasing to the Lord, but did it reluctantly.

He went to war against the Edomites and won, but he brought their idols back with him and set them up and worshipped them, which made the Lord God angry. So God sent a prophet to Amaziah who demanded why he had worshipped foreign gods. Amaziah was going to kill the prophet, but the prophet turned and told the king that *God had decided to destroy him. 2 Chronicles 25:14.*

Many times, the man has seen people walking away from God. Why? When God supplies all their needs and loves them so much that He gave His only son for them, why can they not see? So, we must pray that God will open their eyes to Him, their God.

Jesus said, when he cleaned out the temple of dealers and money changers, *that God's house is a house of prayer.* We are the temple of the Holy Spirit, so we have to be a house of prayer. We need to come together to worship God and Jesus. We do not need wonderful buildings to come together with one voice. We need to worship from our hearts wherever we come together and there are lots of places that God created for this.

Jeremiah 29: 11-13; "I alone know the plans I have for you, plans to bring you prosperity and not disaster, plans to bring about the future you hope for. Then you will call to Me. You will come and pray to Me, and I will answer you. You will seek Me, and you will find Me. Because you will seek Me with all your heart."

2 Chronicles 30:15 tells us that on the fourteenth day of the second month the Passover lamb was killed to sanctify the people, to cleanse them. In our western calendar the fourteenth of February is Valentine's Day is a day where we can show our partners how much we love them. I say that we should show our love to them every day. The same goes for our God. Today, we do not have to kill a lamb. All we have to do is bend a knee and come before Him in repentance to be cleansed of our sins and to show God that we love him very much.

Jesus said that He was in the Father and that the Father was in Him. If we believe in Them, then we too, are in the Father and the Son and we are filled with the Holy Spirit.

John 15:16; "You did not choose me; I chose you and appointed you to go and bear much fruit" This is because Jesus is the vine and we are now part of the vine; branches that will be fed through God's Word. So, if we do not continue to be in the vine and do not bear fruit, then God will trim the bad wood off. God wants us to bear good fruit so we must dwell in His love so that the fruit of the spirit will grow. Then the people will see the abundances of blessings that God, the Father and Jesus, our Lord has given us. Then we can be proclaimers of God's Word and food for others.

When we are part of the vine and are walking with God, men of the earth will try to cut us off the vine, as they tried to do with Jesus, but failed because Jesus conquered the grave. Fear of man can be a snare. *Proverbs 29:25 tells us that it is dangerous to be concerned with what others think of us. If we trust the Lord, we are safe.*

There have been many times where Satan has used people to take the man away from His God. Looking back through some of his old notes on *Philippians 4:9*, marked in his NIV Bible on 23/10/1990:

Philippians 4:9; "If anything is excellent or praiseworthy think about such things, whatever you have learned or received or heard from me, or seen in me, put it into practice and the God of peace will be with you."

And 4:13b says: "I can do anything through Him who gives me strength."

And 4:19: "… and my God will meet all your needs according to His glorious riches, in Christ Jesus."

This was over 26 years ago, and the man can see that God has been working in his life. For many, many, years he was not walking with God or Jesus or the Holy Spirit. It took God to touch him and speak to him before the man was aware of the Trinity. Three words came to him from these passages: peace, strength, and needs and he had seen that God had provided him with all of them. The word of God is pure.

Psalm 12:7 tells us that the words of the Lord are pure words, purified seven times, like silver tried in a furnace on earth.

What would God have in store for him next? And would he be obedient? What gate would God take him through now? With the man's two prayer partners in the church prayer room, as one would pray, he would be given a picture. While they were lifting up the sick, he saw an angel flying over the sick that they were praying for. Then he saw a white horse with its rider. He believed that it was Jesus, also going to the sick to heal them.

The very next day in his prayer time, he saw a picture of two horses pulling a chariot but it was not harnessed to the horses. The driver was a very tall man dressed in the battle dress of ancient times. It did not mean anything to the man, but he wrote it down in his daily notes. Maybe this picture was for the future.

Gate Eighteen

God is a God of humour. The man was fellowshipping with a friend, and was encouraging him in their prayer times. They had a coffee at the café, and talked for a few hours, and the friend told him of his problems in his work and family. As the friend was praying this night, the spirit was talking to the man, and God was asking him what he would do if the hinges on a gate were rusty, and hard to open. The man replied, that he would spray CRC on them and get them working, then oil them with fish oil. *Then God said that we must keep our lives well-oiled, to spray CRC on our lives. The man was taken back. "What" he asked. Then God said, "Yes, Christ's Resurrection's Care".*

Then God explained that the bible needs to be opened every day, to keep us from rusting up, to keep us free, and to keep us working for Gods kingdom. The word of God is important, to keep in God's word, it feeds us and oils us in the Trinity. When the Trinity indwells us we have the full life of God. To get this full life of God we must let go of the old life we had before. We need to ask Jesus into our lives to remove all the sin. Through the Resurrection of Jesus, we are told that we have Eternal life, that Death no longer has dominion over us, so we must be dead indeed to sin, but alive to God.

I would say that there are thousands of Bibles left on shelves, in cupboards, and drawers never opened. There are many, many Christians around the world who do not open their Bibles on a daily basis. *God said, "I'm the A-Z the beginning and the end."* So if the Bible is God's word, then we must read God's word, from the beginning to the end, not skipping pages.

When God, spoke to the man that early morning, and said to the man, "The Gate," nothing more, he locked it in to his mind. The man was a regular bible reader and prayer person, and would be up and about early. It was amazing; he would read a chapter from the Old Testament, a Psalm, a Proverb, and a chapter from the New Testament, this was his regular daily habit.

On this day the Old Testament was Ezekiel 43:1-3. 44:1-3.

V1, afterward he brought me to THE GATE. The gate looks toward the East, V2, and, behold the Glory of the God of Israel came from the way of the east and his voice was like a sound of many waters and the earth shone with his glory.

44: V1, then he brought me back the way of the gate of the outer Sanctuary which looks toward the East and it was shut. V2, and the Lord said to me, this gate will be shut, it will not be opened and no man will enter by it because the LORD, the God of Israel, has entered by it, therefore it will be shut. V3, it is for the Prince, the Prince will sit in it to eat bread before the LORD. He will enter by the way of the porch of that gate and will go out by the way of the same.

Can you see how the man's prayer partners were thinking?

Living near to the town's new development on the eastern side, the man wondered if God was telling him that he was going to be the Gate man Of the east?

Here God is talking to Ezekiel. Was God talking about the Prince of peace, JESUS our Lord and Savior. The saviour of our souls? Ezekiel lived around about 581 BC.

God is always working in advance. The East gate is a very special gate as the God of Israel had been through, and no man will go through. The Prince will sit at the gate. They say that Jesus will return from the East. And many are waiting for his return.

Romans 12:1-2. Paul is telling us. "Therefore, I urge you, brothers, in view of Gods mercy, to offer your bodies as a living sacrifice, Holy and pleasing to God – this is your spiritual act of worship. V2 do not conform any longer to the pattern of this world, but be transformed by the renewing of your mind. Then you will be able to test and approve what God's will is- his good, pleasing and perfect will of God for you."

The Key Hole in the Gate.

We must always look for the key to the gate of the presence of the Trinity: Father, Son, and Spirit, the key is in God's (the Father's) hands. To take the key, we must come closer to the Trinity, we must dwell in His word, to live in His will. Jesus said, "Seek and you will find, knock and the gate will be opened, partake and you will be healed."

59

Psalm 43:3. O send out your light and your truth let them lead me, let them bring me to your Holy mountain, to the place where you dwell.

The Holy mountain is where we will worship the Trinity, in spirit and in truth. It is the only place of peace and we will not get the key by our own works but by *(Psalm 44:4b. The One New Man Bible) the light of God and his Countenance. Because he favoured us, and he is the Way, the Truth, and the Life. The light of the World. AMEN.*

In some Bible translations *Romans 15:6 says: 'one mind.' 'others say 'one heart' and 'one mouth.' Some even say, 'one voice:' that we should glorify the God and Father of our Lord (Y'SHUA) Jesus the Messiah with one voice.* When we come together in prayer and worship, we start to come together with each other in one mind, voice and one heart. Then the spirit takes over and the spirit leads us on to lift others up to God, to support the weak. We are bonded to the Trinity, and God speaks through the spirit and takes us down the right path, we are not pleasing ourselves, we are as one.

1 Corinthians, 3:9. Tells us that we are cultivated fields of God, a building of God, so one must plant the seed and one water. But it is God who makes it grow, the one that waters and the one that plants are equal. We must not turn away the humble: but encourage them. Let us not sow weeds but to continue to cultivate the fields of God, with the spirit of God, the spirit of God will cultivate us more and more with God's spiritual teaching and they (we) will discern all things by the spirit and we are of the Messiah Jesus, in Him we will trust, to be more cultivated and humble ourselves to God the Holy one.

One Sunday morning God gave the man a picture of a waterfall: a large waterfall. *God said to go over the waterfall: that the hole at the bottom is where the water is collected before going further downstream. When we are there the spirit will flood over us, filling us more and more with the spirit. This is a time when all people will be filled with the spirit of God and be Holy.*

1 Corinthians 6: 17. But the one who is joined to the Lord is one spirit with him.

The man was thinking to himself, but I have been baptized in the Holy Spirit: how much more can we take? Is it that when we pour out the spirit on others, that God keeps filling us up, it was as if God was saying,

As you pond at the bottom of the waterfall, the spirit fills us, then when it is time God moves us down the river to be used by God himself. We may not travel far downstream to a path God has for us and takes us along. What we have to do is in Micah 6: 8.

To be imitators of Jesus the Messiah YES!!

To be imitators of Demons NO!!

We must walk in the light of Jesus our Lord, to show others the way, to share the grace of Jesus, giving God the Glory and blessings. Jesus said to love the Lord God with all our hearts, souls, minds, and all our strength, and love others as ourselves. The word humble as in Micah 6:8, we must humble ourselves before God to bend a knee, to come humbly before God. To be meek and submissive, to go into the Holy of Holies, then God will take us further down the stream, where God will use us in shallower waters and could be the next gate for us, before taking us further downstream in God's timing. This may be a time of teaching from God: teaching us to walk humbly with your God. Micah 6:8.

The man was with a friend called John, who he was encouraging. God said to the man that *He (God) would build him up, and thought of a wall. "No," God said, "a net." God was saying that John would be a net across the stream and would catch people who would come down John's stream.* These included his work mates and other people he came in contact with. If his net got holes in it, John would have to fix them. This brought back memories for the time from the past, when God told him in a vision of the net: that He would be a net across the man's stream, that he would have to make sure that there were no holes in his net. The man started to think back many, many years: when God had plans for him years before !!WOW!!

Do you have a journal? Start one today and write down what God says to you. You will be amazed when you read it years later, sometimes it may not be for you but to encourage someone else.

God gave us Jesus, Jesus gave us the spirit, the spirit gave us the fruits and gifts: nine fruits of the spirit to live by.

Galatians 5: 16, Gifts of the spirit to work for God by. In 1 Timothy 4:6-16 it gives us encouragement and commands us to keep in God's word, to never neglect the spiritual gifts, and that we should regularly cultivate these spiritual gifts, that we must occupy ourselves with reading, exhortation, and teaching, giving thanks always and we must be always in the word, conduct, love, faith and purity. To continue to seek true Holiness with God to encourage each other as the Father speaks to us and as we pray, we go deeper into his presence, we must continue to work on the rusty hinges of the gate of Holiness and we must walk in the (CRC) Christ's Resurrection Care. All the time spraying the fish oil of God on others.

The man was praying with one of his prayer partners when God gave him a picture of the prayer partner, and the man in a flame (the man said it looked like a candle flame), that he could see the two of them walking in the flame, (this is not the first time that the man has been in this flame or fire with others walking to the Altar of God). (Could this be the gate that God had spoken about the first time?) The man said he was overwhelmed by the presence of the Trinity, to know that he was with them in the Holy of Holies. God asked the him "who have you got with you." The man would tell God. At that time, he would be moved into praying in the spirit at God's Alter.

Gate Nineteen

Joseph already had a dream about the sheaves of wheat. As the sheaves of wheat were stood up by his brothers, all the brothers sheaves of wheat bowed before Joseph's. As Joseph told them the dream, they were all up in arms about it, even his father wasn't happy about the dream. The brothers had to get rid of Joseph.

When we read about Joseph, he was sold as a slave not knowing God's plan for him. He was put into jail, but God used him to interpret dreams, he had to wait upon the Lord, till the word came from the Lord God to purify him, or you may say, a time of teaching. Psalm 105:17-19 You see God sets the time for our word, as the song goes (in his time he makes all things beautiful) and he did for Joseph, he took him from the jail, to one of the top jobs in Egypt. We could say that we need God in our life. The man would say that he wanted God the Trinity in his life for they are the Truth. You could say, to be obedient to Him that he gives joy, love, and peace and to others strength and healing. Knowing God is our supplier, He gives us all things, without God (the Trinity) we are just dust, we are the fertilizer for other things to grow.

Hebrews 3:7-15. V15b If you would hear His voice today do not harden your hearts as in the rebellion.

When we hear God's voice our lives are turned around. Take Saul. He was persecuting the believers of God and Jesus, putting them in jail and killing some, but God stepped in and used His (God's) power of light, threw Saul to the ground, and blinding him. God then spoke to him and Saul answered, and said, "Who is this?" and Jesus said, "It is I, Jesus of Nazareth, the one you are persecuting." Saul was blinded for three days and God sent Ananias to pray over Saul. Ananias was afraid he did not want to go through that gate but God said, "You must do this because this person is a chosen vessel for Me." God was opening the gate, Ananias had to go through, also opening a new gate in Saul's life, and Saul would not have known the persecution and gates, that God was going to take him through for God's glory. So God healed Saul's eyes, and also blessed him with the Holy Spirit, and changed his name to Paul, the gate of building God's church up, and not pulling it down.

David the shepherd boy, was also was a chosen vessel for God. David had a giant at one of his gates: he heard words from the giant, words that defiled David's God, so David knew he had to go through that gate. Nothing was going to stop him, the thing was David did not know that his God was going to open many, many more gates in his life, and all for God's glory. David had the Holy Spirit in him, that give him the boldness and power of God to slay the giant. David became a great king over God's people.

So are you a chosen vessel? The man is now coming to realize that he is a chosen vessel that God has already opened many gates, but still not knowing what path God is taking him on. When we read God's word we are told to fear God, if we walk and talk with God, why fear someone that loves us so much? He (God) created us in his image, he has given us the Holy Spirit to know the right way to live, the right things to do which will not anger God, but to love him and love others as he loves us.

Deuteronomy 10:20, You will revere the Lord your God. You will serve Him and you will cleave to Him and swear by His name. v21 He is your praise and He is your God, who has done great and awesome things for you.

The man and his wife had the opportunity to travel to Israel. On this particular day he traveled to the Jordan river.

They had a young boy in their group who was going to be baptized. Before the boy got into the water the spirit was prompting the man, (maybe a song), but the pastor of the group said that we would sing a song after the baptism. The man thought that's ok but what is the spirit going to do through him, as he knew that the spirit was working in him. After the boy was baptized one of the group prayed over the boy then through the spirit in the man, he prophesied over the boy.

As the man had his eyes closed he could see darts of light coming down on the young boy, the Spirit then said that the boy was being filled with the light, that the Spirit would work in him and do great things in him, that he will work in the supernatural, and he will be well protected by the Spirit. The Spirit was speaking in tongues for the man to interpret, this was for the boy and the whole group to know.

The next day the group visited an orphanage which was right next door to their hotel. The group was guided to a lovely small chapel. As the group entered, the Spirit started to work on the man, the spirit was prompting him to sing a song of thanksgiving to God, not knowing the rule of the chapel he asked the leader to ask for permission. This was given so the Spirit spoke to him and said, "Get the group to sit down and face the Cross." The spirit led the man in a spiritual tongue that was so powerful, that as he had his hands high with his fingers spread wide, it was as though electricity was going through his fingers. He was saying that there was real power within him and that he did not think that this had happened to him before. Let it be the Lord God Amen.

The man could see that, just as Jesus felt the power going from him, when the woman with the blood problem was healed just by touching the prayer shawl of Jesus. That was what he felt in the chapel: like the power of Jesus, he said that he felt that if he had touched someone that they would have been zapped by God's power.

So the man wants to encourage you to keep in God's word and as close as you can to the Trinity: the Father, the Son and the Holy Spirit. To walk with Them daily, to continually talk to them, the three in one. You will be amazed at what God will do through you and the places He (God) will take you in the spirit. This is not about the man, it's about what God, our Lord has done through him. *In Deuteronomy 17:18-20, v18. And it will be when he sits on the throne of his Kingdom, that he will write a copy of this Torah in a scroll out of that which is before the priests, the Levites. V19. And it will be with him and he will read from it all the days of his life, so he can learn to revere the LORD his God, to keep all the words of this Torah and these statutes, to do them V20, so his heart will not be lifted up above his brothers and so he does not turn aside from the commandment to the right hand or to the left: to the end that he may prolong his days in his kingdom, he and his children, in the midst of Israel,"*

The Spirit spoke to the man and was saying that this is God's word that God is the alpha and omega, so this is not just for kings. It's for all God's children: You and Me.

The man recalls a time he was in Israel on the tour, when they were visiting some churches where Jesus would have ministered. While the man was praying, the Spirit took him along seeing mountains and hills as it was in the time of Jesus. The spirit took him deep into the earth and in different directions. The man then asked himself was this for him or others that we should search ourselves deeper for sin to be cleaned out, so the spirit can come deeper into us?

In the second church, as the man was praying he saw himself in a very dark cave, to the left of the cave was Jesus, in a wonderful ray of light, and he was in the picture till he opened his eyes.

The third church, The Church of Mark, was run by a woman. As the man met her she sang a song, and he started to get pictures: first the side of a man's head with white hair and beard, then other pictures: it was just like a slide show. Was he interpreting the song? Was this a new season? A new gate? Was God opening a new Gate of interpretation for him? Was the man ready to go through? Maybe the man did not want to go through, maybe the man needed more of Christ's Resurrections Care to trust in the Trinity. We must listen to the Holy Spirit, like a person that plays an instrument to the timing and the beat, also the sound of our hearts that beat stronger to the Spirit's call and the Holy Spirit opens the gate to prophesying and healing, or it may be a song of thanksgiving to God.

There is nothing to be afraid of if that gate is opened to you. The Holy Spirit will do the work. It may be the help gate to help someone who is in trouble or lost. Jesus came to save the lost, and when we are in Jesus, Jesus is in us. Maybe you are the gate for that person to come to know Jesus, as their Lord and Saviour. Jesus said that he is the shepherd, but we become the shepherd to open the gate.

Sometimes the Spirit would give the man a message for someone. While on the trip to Israel he was given a message for one of the Irish girls about her smile, the spirit said to him to tell her that her smile was a contagious smile, that she must not let anyone take it away, that it's a smile of Jesus and a smile of love. The man passed it on and she thanked the man but the thanks goes to God's Spirit. *Hebrews 3:7, On this account, just as the Holy Spirit says, "Today if you hear His voice. Do not harden your hearts as in the rebellion. 4:1, says, therefore we should take care lest we would in any way depart from a promise to enter his rest. V3, for we who have believed enter the rest, just as he has said. So we must go through a gate to God's rest, reading on in V11 it says to make every effort to enter that eternal rest. God said on the seventh day He (God) rested from all his works.*

Proverbs 8: 33, Listen to instruction! Be wise! Do not refuse it! V34, Blessed is the man who hears me, watching daily at my Gates, waiting at the posts of my doors. So God is saying there are many gates and many doors to go through, we say love is the key, God says he who loses the keys of the kingdom on earth, will lose the keys in heaven, where is God taking him now?

The man was listening to a CD and the spirit was saying, "Keys"

Forgiveness.

Faith.

Blessings to others.

We will be taken through gates if we have the right KE: Father, Son, and Spirit. When we listen and God speaks to us, and we hear and obey, then we start to go through the gate, we will have the key to open the right gate. Will it be the key of forgiveness, faith or blessing to others? God will supply all our needs to walk that path through the gates.

Psalm 9:14b, you who lifts me up from the gates of Death, V15 so I can tell of all your praises in the gates of the daughter of Zion. I will rejoice exuberantly in your deliverance!

If we are in a place with high walls and locked gates, NO KEYS, a place with no one around, how and who is going to help us get out and where do we go? Which key is it Forgiveness? Faith? Blessings to others? Or do we call on the Trinity? Father, Son or Spirit? (we sing a song called, I will call upon the Lord) Jesus was the key when He (Jesus) opened the gate for us to go into the Holy of Holies, the gate with the curtain ripped in two. We can get the key by prayer and praise (worship). Spending time with the Father, Son and Spirit. This is where the key is keeping in tune with God.

Acts 12:6, Peter was sleeping in prison between two soldiers, bound with two chains and there were guards by each door, guarding the prison, V7, and behold an angel of the Lord stood and a light shone out in the prison: and as he struck Peter's side he woke him up. V10b, and they came upon the iron gate leading into the city, which was open to them by itself.

This is the mighty power of God unlocking the chains, and unlocking the doors and gate without waking any of the soldiers. The power of God to do these things. *V5 tell us that there was fervent prayer to God being made by the congregation concerning him(Peter).* And God heard their prayers, the people opened the gate to God, and God opened the gate to release Peter into the street, (nothing is impossible to God). So when we come together with other prayer people God speaks. One night in the prayer room the man recalls that he was prostrate on the floor as the other partner was praying. The man was facing the carpet which had just been fitted. God said to him, "Do you see--- the carpet and how it had been woven and how tight it was?" And he said in reply how could he miss it as he was only a nose away. God said that this is the way He (God) wants his church tightly woven so it would be strong, so it would be together and will wear well and stand up for his Kingdom. The next day the man was talking to one of the other prayer partners sharing the word from God. He started to laugh, then the prayer partner shared what God had said to him that morning about the carpet binding, that keeps the carpet from fraying that is how God keeps his people together, and how God talks to us.

They also talked about onions, how when you peel them you get to another layer of skin, and how God peels the skins off us (the things we do not need) and teaches us things he wants us to know and learn. There was a member of the man's church, a very nice older lady well-learned in the scriptures, who asked him one day, where did he get his teaching from, and who had been teaching him. After a short time, the man said it must be God. The lady asked which Bible college did he go to, the man replied none. So it must be that when you walk and talk with God daily, God is teaching us every day: every time we pray.

Deuteronomy 7:1 God is speaking to the Israelites about when they go into the promised land, that God was going to give them and the promise He (God) had made to their fathers, that they are a Holy people to the Lord their God. And he will be with them.

When the Lord your God brings you through the gate, through your life, God leads us to the next gate that He (God) has planned for us.

God does not make us go out from one gate and into another gate, but brings us out and into another gate (let's say that we are at the oppressed gate, God will bring us through that gate and into the forgiveness gate, to forgive our oppressors, then God will take us through the Blessing gate to bless us and others. God does not order, force, make or send, God takes us. But we have the choice whether to go through or not).

God showed his people his mighty power, again God opened the water Gate, the Jordan river in flood, when the priest's feet hit the water the river stopped, so his people could walk through the gate into the promised land, and they walked on dry ground. So God was before them, behind them and at the left and right.

Deuteronomy 6:9 here God talks about his word, his commandments (THE TEN) telling his people to write on the door posts and the gates of our houses, on our hands and foreheads (the gate of life so we will do the right things in life) our gate to a really good life is GOD'S WORD, *the Bible.*

Deuteronomy 11: 20, God speaks to his people.

Psalm 69:13, those who sit in the gate speak against you and you could be the song of the drunkards, these are the people who come against you trying to stop you from doing God's will.

Gate Twenty

The Prayer Gate

We have just been reading about how the congregation were all together praying for Peter, and God heard their prayers. The word tells us, that when two or more are gathered together in prayer, that the Trinity; Father, Son, and Holy Spirit, are there with us, plus the host of angels. How blessed we are, when we open the prayer gate to God.

When in prayer with the Trinity they (the Father, Son, and Spirit) lead us in our prayers, with pictures and words. Many times we will not know what they mean. Sometimes God will speak in a tongue and the spirit will interpret it. This is the Trinity working together, putting a power out that is so powerful, to open prison doors and gates with the power to heal, when we pray from our hearts.

Within the church there is a prayer chain: some people are placed on the chain for healing, or other things. We pray over the problem. Jesus was a great prayer early on a morning, and through the day, he (Jesus) would seek the Father's will. No matter where we are we can pray. We read in the book of Jonah that he was in the belly of the whale, because he, Jonah, went through the wrong gate, the wrong way, but God heard his prayer and made the whale spat him out onto the beach. Judas definitely took the wrong gate. Oops!!

The man would often get a picture of someone, that he may or may not know, being prompted to pray for them: this is intercessory prayer.

Being in prayer is so wonderful and so rewarding, and when God hears your prayer for someone, and gives you a word for them, or tells you something about the one you are praying for, and that person confirms it to you, that is the rewarding part.

Jeremiah 29:11-13, for I AM knows the thoughts, plans, and intentions that I AM thinking toward you, says the Lord, thoughts of peace and not of evil, to give

70

you a future and hope. V12. Then you will call upon Me and you will go and PRAY to Me and I shall heed you. v13, and you will seek ME and find Me. When you will search for me with all your heart.

The Lord God loves our thanks and praise and much more from us. The Bible tells us that the wise men took two years to find Baby Jesus. How long and how far are you prepared to go in your search for God?

When we get to the gate, which may be shut, do we turn back and slide away from God, or do we persist in our prayers till the gate is opened for us by God. No matter where we are, God is not far away from us. When we sit, walk, sleep, work, drive and eat, God is right there with us. He does all the things we do, when we give our all to Him, we are one with him, Amen!!

When we read Esther3:1-, we read about the King's gate: this was the time God opened the gate, for him to rule God's people. Now a man called Haman was setting out to bring the death gate to all of God's people. Esther and Mordecai would not worship this King, they were steadfast in their worship: to the one true God, the God of all creation.

Mordecai sat many days at the King's gate, not looking forward to the death gate Haman was setting for him. Esther and Mordecai agreed to get all God's people to fast and pray, and God locked the death gate, and no one could open it: so when we trust in God, evil will not prevail. God is the gate keeper of our lives. When we trust in Him (God), the right gate will be opened to us, as God did for Mordecai: as he was given the top job: the King's right-hand man. And God opened the death gate to Haman. We see what corporate prayer can achieve: the Power of prayer.

Now a new gate for Mordecai had opened, he had gone through the captive gate, to create a new life for the Jews, as God closed the death gate, and opened the life gate. God can open our creative gate when we trust and follow him: When we open our heart gate, our prayer gate, our worship gate.

Psalm 103:1-6, we read David said, "bless the Lord, O my soul! All that is with in me, bless his Holy name, V2, Bless the Lord, O my soul! Do not forget all his benefits! V3, who forgives all your iniquities! Who heals all our diseases! V4, who redeems your life from destruction! Who crowns you with loving kindness, and compassion! V5, who satisfies your old age with good things, so that your youth is renewed like the eagle's"

One Sunday morning, in the church service, the Lord gave the man a picture of a gold ring, with 4 diamond stones set in it. God asked him, *"are my people engaged to me?"* The man was taken aback and started to think that when two people get engaged there is a ring to show what they have done.

So when we are engaged to God, we must show it in our lives what we have done, that we are one with God, Jesus, and the Holy Spirit: then we can say *bless the Lord O my soul and bless his Holy name. Psalm 103:1*

In the book of Ester 8:2, we read that Mordecai was given the king's ring, and it gave him the king's power: a lot of power! The people could see the king's ring, and they were obedient to do what Mordecai had ordered.

So we are seeing the power of prayer, and how God opens the gates for the prayer warriors. Daniel was a prayer warrior: on his knees three and four times every day worshipping God.

Daniel 2:49, tells us that Daniel also sat in the King's gate. God opened the gate of interpreting dreams for the King. The King that Daniel was under did not follow God, but wanted to be the only God. In 2: 37, of the book of Daniel it says the God of heaven had given the King his kingdom, power, and strength and his glory. (God is the gate keeper). We must wait on the Lord God to open the right gate, just like Daniel waited, and prayed and God opened the gate of interpretation of dreams, opened the gate, to the fear of God to the King.

Not only was Daniel in prayer, but also his three friends; Shadrach, Meshach and Abednego, blocking the death gate. All four were in prayer. They had faith in God, for in the word of God it says, *"Fear not for I AM with you."* So we must open the ear gate, and listen to the Spirit.

Ephesians 5:18b, but you must continually be filled with the Spirit, V20, giving thanks to our God and Father, always, for all things in the name of our Lord Y'shua Messiah (Jesus).

Ephesians 5:21 being subject to one another, Wife and Husband, so God takes us through the congregation gate. When we come to the Lord our God, we join others in worship to God, and we come into corporate prayers. Jesus said to love one another like I have loves you, going through the congregation gate. We may be locked into it or by it, God puts us into the congregation field, to see how we cope with each other, and how we love one another. And to encourage each other, praying together, also to take others through the gate. This may be the encouraging gate, or a teaching gate.

How long are we in each gate? in the congregation gate? is *God saying wait there till I send more of the Holy Spirit,* we may try and jump the gate. Or do we continue to encourage others? Are we a Barnabas or Paul or Peter? Whatever your name God could change that.

The man recalls, an incident that happened many years ago as he was in the building trade. He was called on to do some building work for a church friend. As the work was finished, he placed the account for the work which had been done. (This had not been quoted for,) The owner said it was higher than the quoted cost, that the man was ripping him off. The man was very upset at being called a liar and the friend would not pay the full amount.

Some weeks later the man was driving past the friend's shop, and there was another builder working there. The man got very angry, that the friend had got someone else to do his work. The man prayed to God about it, *then God spoke to him saying, "do not be angry. I will shut the gate, so you will not get hurt again." These things come to show us that God is always with us.*

Proverbs 24: 19, Do not fret Yourself because of bad people! Do not envy the wicked! V 20, for there will be no future for the bad one: the lamp of the wicked will be put out.

Psalm 24:7, Lift up your heads, O you gates and be lifted up, you everlasting doors, and the King of Glory will come in.

So the Lord our God is saying that we are a gate, an everlasting door. You are the gate for others to enter, to lead them to the King of Glory. You may ask, "Who is the King of Glory?" he is the Lord God: strong and mighty. So when we give ourselves to God, the Trinity, we are gates and doors for God, and we are everlasting, from the beginning to the everlasting in God's Kingdom: from your father's seed to everlasting. Amen.

We see from above that there is an Evil Gate, and a Wisdom gate. We are not to oppress the oppressed, nor push them away: but help them, at the time at their gate. The Lord is with them, and will protect them. If we spoil them, then God will spoil our souls: He will plead their cause.

Proverbs 22:22-23.

God made us in his image, so we can have a relationship with him, and come close to Him. The Bible is full of people, who have had a close relationship with God himself. Has God revealed himself to you YET?

Psalm 28:1

David cried out to God, "Do not be silent to me," He had a close, two-way relationship with God.

Once, As the man was repairing a timber deck, which had been painted brown, it started to rain. As he sat and watched, three or four raindrops landed on the deck, but dried up with the heat of the day. A few more landed but also dried up. As the rain got heavier there were more drops, and the timber was starting to get wetter, and not drying up, till all the timber was wet and the water was running off it.

The Lord God then said to him through the raindrops, *"The more of my people that come to pray together, the more the Spirit will move." Two or three in prayer dry up. God wants to have more and more people in prayer.*

In the prayer room at the church, God gave the man two pictures: one picture was an open book which was the Bible. God said, "1John." Then the second picture was of a metronome on a piano. The man was taken aback and wondered what God was saying. Then God gave him a song, from 1962 called *'listen to the rhythm of the falling rain'. The man shared the pictures and the song with his other prayer partners. God said to listen to the rhythm of His (God's) words, His voice, His whisper, to keep in rhythm with His voice, like the metronome keeps the beat.* If we go too fast, then we are out of beat with His (God's) word: if we go slower, we have to catch up with His word.

74

We must always keep the beat in rhythm with God. (The man thinks that this is another gate?).

1 John 3:24 says he who keeps God's commandments, remains in Him, and He in us, and by this we know that He (God) remains in us, by the spirit whom He gave to us.

Numbers 25, Psalm 51, Job 23, 1Cor 9:13, All these readings take us through different gates, so we keep reading Gods Word. So we receive the right teaching on how to live and how to come before God in prayer.

1 Corinthians 9:13, those who officiate in the Temple rites ate from the Holy things of the temple.

So when we come before God in prayer and his word, we are eating of God's goodness.

Some who serve regularly at the alter have a share in the alter, so when we come regularly in prayer to God's alter we have shares in the alter to (we are in God as God is in us).

When we are in prayer we must continually lift our children up to God to keep them safe. *We read in Job 5:4 how Job's children were taken from him crushed in the death gate.* We do not know if they followed their father in the ways of God or was it because Satin was after Job? This was a way he could get at Job. Let's put it this way, if we are away from God are we safe?

So if we have gone through the wrong gate, who is there to lead us back to the safety of God? The word tells us that we are a speck of dust, (a grain of sand) that God holds us in the palm of His hand. God loves us so much that He wants us to be in Him and HE in us. God does not want to be in the other room, God wants to be in our hearts always to walk and talk with Him.

Romans 10:12, for there is no distinction between either Jewish or Greek, for the same one is Lord of all, and He is rich, abundantly blessing all those who call upon Him: V 13 for everyone who calls upon the name of the Lord will be saved.

When we read Job 29:7 when I went out to the gate through the city, I prepared my seat in the street! He would be there to welcome people to the city.

We could call this the help gate, have you been at this gate helping others, being there for them, praying for them, visiting the sick?

We have been reading about Job he lost everything children, all his stock, (sheep, cows, donkeys, everything) all he was left with was his wife. He's going through the poor gate, the oppressed gate. But still keeps his eyes on his GOD. Job is saying if he has done wrong he will take the punishment from God.

The man recalls a time at his friends home in a prayer time, God showed him a picture of an oil painters palette, where he mixes the paint for the painting. God also showed him a picture, of a crystal cutter and a potter, God was saying to him that the painter, the cutter, and the potter, had their designs ready to start their creation. The painter mixed the paint colors to start, the crystal cutter marks out his design on the glass ready for the diamond cutter, the potter gets the clay ready for the wheel. All three are ready to work on their creation and to finish them.

God was saying to the man that He is the three, the painter, crystal cutter, and the potter, and we are the paint, glass and clay. That He God, is making us in to what He wants us to be like, moulding us into himself, (that's how we are in Him and He in us) He's the painter moving the brush to create the picture. God paints colors into our lives, (the moods in us how we mix with others, the more paint the more we stand out He smooths us out so we blend in with others).

He's the cutter when He starts with our design, we are plain see through glass, as each movement the cutter cuts the glass (sometimes He will have to cut deeper, and sometimes not so deep) but each cut is as He wants it to be. God polishes us to shine as the sun or light hits the cuts, it reflects the light and different colors. We are the glass, canvas, and the clay, and if we let God the creator do His work in us we will be that beautiful person He (God) wanted us to be. Showing others God's wonderful colors, reflecting His light through us, and a beautiful shape that will attract others to Himself. So we can be in Him and He in us, can you be ready to be moulded. Let me put it this way, will you let Him mould you?

Lifting the Veil.

2 Corinthians 3:13. In life, we sometimes go around with a veil over our heads, (just like Moses after being with God). He had a veil over his head because his face was so bright the people couldn't look at him for the spirit of God was in him, do you have a veil over you? let Jesus the

Messiah remove it today. Let God's spirit work through you and in you don't hide behind that veil be bold go through the gate. God needs you to keep your eyes on Y'SHUA (Jesus), and it will be a great joy to you and others when you are filled with the Holy Spirit, your face will be so bright you will draw people to the Trinity Amen.

Gate Twenty-One

Galatians 3:26 These verses tell us that when we go through Baptism (immersed in water), into the Messiah, we go through the gate being washed of the water, and cleansed from our sin. So we are going from the sin gate washed by the blood of Jesus our Messiah, by faith we are one with Y'SHUA (Jesus). We become the seed. You have been clothed with the Messiah.

Abraham a new life with the promises of God.

Heirs in the Kingdom.

We must keep ourselves from going back through the sin gate, and any other gate that is still open to wrong doing.

Deuteronomy 12: God talks about His statutes and judgments so we can have a good life, our offerings to God are everything we have.

Our thanks giving, our praise, worship, prayers, and our fellowship with Him. God tells us to listen to him carefully. The Bible tells us that we must walk in the spirit, live by the spirit, love by the spirit, and be led by the spirit. In the next chapter *God is talking about our gates, about the strangers that are in our gates, 14: 21,* The fatherless, the widows within our gates, the increase we lay up within our gates, *Deuteronomy 14:28.*

All these things come to us in different times of our lives so these Scriptures are teaching us (God's Torah).

Deuteronomy 10: 20, You will revere the Lord your God. You will serve him and you will cleave to him, and swear by his name. V 21 He is your praise, and he is your God.

Our offerings (tithings) are wages for the priests, loving and helping others, fatherless children, our worship, our thanks giving, helping the poor, the sick, our prayers encouragement to others, all these things come to us at different times of our lives, these are different gates.

When we read Ruth 2: 10 about the stranger, she was a stranger and she found favor in Boaz and he let her glean in his fields, this was because she was looking after her mother in law. This was part of Boaz's tithings to God, our tithes are all that we do for God.

And God takes us through the Blessing Gate. (Ephesians 1:3-2, there are more gates). It's not 10% tithing its 100% of ourselves every part of us. Every gate God takes us through prepares us for the kingdom of heaven, God's Place. V 3, Blessed be God and father of our Lord Y'shua Messiah, the one who blessed us with every spiritual blessing in the heavenlies by the Messiah. V20, which he worked in the Messiah when he raised Him from the dead, and He seated Him on His right hand in the heavenlies. 2: V5b, you have been saved by grace, 2: V15 so that He could create the two, Jewish and non-Jewish into ONE NEW MAN establishing peace.

Deuteronomy 15:7 Here God is saying if there is any poor man with you, one of your brothers within any of your gates. In your land which the Lord your God gives you. You will not harden your heart or shut your hand from your poor brother. V8, That we are to care for them. God also says in this passage about our heart gate, and our thought gate, V9, Beware of any wicked thoughts in your heart.

Ruth was in the poor gate and Boaz blessed her. *In the book of Ruth 4:13, God takes Ruth through another gate this is the gate of marriage to Boaz. 4:16, as God puts the seed in her for a child which they named him Obed, who was the father of Jesse. He was the father of David who became King David.* Through this story we can see how God works in our lives. *If Naomi's husband and two sons had not died, Naomi and her two daughters-in-laws widows,* they would not have moved back to the land of Judah to where her kinsmen lived, there may not have been a King David.

So we can see that God was with them and it was God's plan for them. We can look at our lives and know that God has a plan for us all, before birth and after death right through our lives. Follow God and do the right thing for God is in control and it is for God's purpose.

King Solomon (The Preacher) in Ecclesiastes 3:1-22 he talks about the seasons, a time for all things for every purpose for everything, (like the gates we must go through in our life time as we walk with God), it's all God's teaching through His Book. This should be like the gates in our lives that God opens and shuts the Bible.

Colossians 3:4 When we read this chapter it's like a new season we go through, we have stripped off the old man with his deeds. We become a book for God that we are easy to read and the peace of the Messiah, must continually rule in our hearts as it says in this chapter, we must love each other as Jesus loves us. It's a new season, a new gate, this is the only way we can go taking God's path and have a good and wonderful life with the Father, Son, and Spirit. When we change for the good we must be strong, *(just as God said to Joshua be strong! Be of good courage!* Was this the biggest gate that Joshua would go through?) read Joshua 1: God also said *Do not be dismayed! For the Lord your God is with you.*

We must listen to God's Spirit, and not to men, for God is the gate keeper of all things. "We sing trust and obey for there is no other way to be happy in Jesus is to trust and obey".

Deuteronomy 27:9, we read about Moses and the priests, the Levites spoke to all Israel saying silence! Listen! Obey, O Israel! This day you have become the people of the Lord your God. V10, Moses continues to tell the people you will therefore obey the voice of the Lord your God, and do his Commandments, and his statutes which I command you this day.

Psalm 87:.2, The Lord loves the gates of Zion, more than all the dwellings of Jacob.

Psalm 88:2, The psalmist is crying out to God, for God to incline his ear to the prayers of the psalmist who is crying out for the fellowship with God. The fellowship Gate.

We need to come before God every day to listen, to be silent, to be obedient to God. That we cry out to God like the Psalmist, *the word tells us that obedience is better than sacrifice. 1 Samuel 15:22.*

Ecclesiastes 4:17 says, watch your step when you go to the house of God and be more ready to listen than to give the sacrifice of fools for they do not consider that they do evil. There are many many scriptures in the Torah (God's Word) the teachings of God.

The man was recalling a time when in prayer with God part of the prayer was that the man only wanted the mark of his God. The man's reading that day was from:

Deuteronomy 28:58 Through this chapter there is lots of warnings about the curses and lots of blessings. V58, if you will not observe to do all the words of this Torah that is written in the scroll so you will revere this glorious and awesome name the Lord your God. I can see, the only way is to keep in the Torah, to walk and talk with our Lord God, Amen.

We are encouraged to stay faithful to God, Jesus and the Holy Spirit. If we go through distress and afflictions we must have faith in God. Establish our hearts blameless in holy before our God. To be clean and keep our eyes on God.

In the old song it says "man will live forever more because of Christmas day". Well there is a catch to that man will live for evermore but we must follow and do God's teachings, God's Commandments, God's Statues, giving ourselves Holy to God, Son and Spirit. That is every part of us to the Trinity so we cross into a covenant with the Lord our God, and into his oath which the Lord our God cuts with us this day.

We must be watchful to always be in prayer to God, to put on the breastplate of faith, love, the helmet and the hope of salvation. God did not put us here to be subject to WRATH, but to gain salvation through Y'SHUA Messiah, (Jesus our Lord), we must put on the full armor of God each day. We must meet with God the Father, Son and Holy Spirit each day and humble ourselves before Him. God does not ask us for much but gives us all we need.

Quite a few chapters in the bible God takes us through many gates, the watching gate, love gate, faith gate, and hope gate. Putting on the full armor of God this is God's word from the first page to the last page.

Deuteronomy 31: 12 Gather the people together men, women, children and your strangers that is within your Gates, so they can hear and so they will learn and revere the Lord our God and observe, to do all the words of his teaching.

What Gates is God talking about here at this time. Israel was at the side of the river Jordan before going into the Promise Land (there's no gates as such). Is God talking about the gates of our lives? So the children may hear God and learn to revere the Lord our God. So again we come back to the bible God's teaching the Torah. We are at the learning gate, listening gate, the blessing gate. God wants to bless us all as He wanted to bless His people when they crossed the Jordan River to the promise land.

God was with them. He opened the gate stopped the river so His people could go through on dry land and not wet their feet. God was to do more wonders for them when they arrived at the prayer gate.

Jeremiah 29: 11-13 For I AM, knows the thoughts, plans, and intentions, that I AM thinking toward you, says the Lord, thoughts of peace, and not evil, to give you a future and hope, v12 then you will call upon Me, and you will go and pray to Me, and I shall heed you, v13 and you will seek Me, and fined Me, then you will search for Me with your heart.

When you pray "I will listen". If you look for Me, whole heartedly you, "will find Me" the wise still seek God's face, to talk with Him, and give all that they have to Him, thanks giving and praise and much more. The wise men took two years to find Baby Jesus. How long and how far are you prepared to go in your search for God? We can get to the gate which may be shut.

Do we turn back and slide away from God or do we persist in our prayers till the gate is opened for us by God? God is not far away from you when you sit, walk, sleep, work, drive, and listen. God is right there with you, He does all the things you do when we give our all to Him, we are one with him Amen.

Psalm 107: 1-22. The writer is telling us, to worship God, to thank Him, to keep in rhythm with God, and God will save us from our troubles and distractions, that only God can, (V 16. break down the gates of bronze, and cuts the bars of iron as under), V14 says, he brought them out of darkness, and the shadow of death, and broke their bonds. And God brings us into the glorious light (Jesus the Messiah).

Daniel 3:19-4: Shows us how God can break down the gates, how He protected, Shadrach, Meshach, and Abednego. God blocked the Death gate, and opened a new gate in their lives, and how God's signs and wonders are mighty and how great and mighty God is when we worship only God and praise him, how mighty His love is towards us.

Hebrews 3-4, tells us about hearing from God, (3:7 just as the Holy Spirit says, today if you would hear His voice), do not harden your hearts as in rebellion.

When we are in the ear gate we must listen to God, through the Holy Spirit and not to be afraid of His voice. In the old testament we read about God speaking to Moses. God said to him to get the people together at the bottom of the mountain so He could speak to them, they came the next day to hear God but when they heard His voice they were afraid. When we hear God's voice we should not be afraid of Him but to listen to Him.

Today with my time with God reading, *Hebrews 6, talks about heavenly gifts, and blessings from God, the word of God, and the power, and works, the foot note for V5 from the One New Man Bible says, (as we are the gifts, we are to expect miracles, to experience the awesome power of God in our everyday lives. We will not have the fullness of the power in this age but we are surely to taste the power. Every saint is to be trained to walk in victory and power in order to bring into the kingdom those who do not have a relationship with God).* This is the gate of the Holy Spirit the gifting Gate, the power gate. Reading this God saying we go through the gifting gate on earth but when our spirits return to God we get the fullness of God's power.

Looking at the trees I see seeds dropping to the ground, dead seeds, but when they land the rain comes and spring arrives, they start a new life, the life gate. They grow into a new tree, they fruit and drop seed and the cycle goes on and on again. God is so awesome he made all of creation (all) to go on and on we come through the seed gate, we grow, we produce seeds, we fruit, we go through many other gates, but only the gates that God has opened for us. The gates He wants us to go through for His kingdom, for His glory, for His purpose, the track we take.

Hebrews 8:10 When I (God) put my teaching into their minds for understanding and I (God) shall write them upon their hearts, and I (God) shall be their God, and they will be my people. So God's word the bible is the teachings we are to read page by page, word for word, to retain it, to live it, to proclaim it.

The gates of righteousness.

Psalm 18:31-33(King David)

As for God, His way is perfect: the word of the Lord is tried: He is a shield to all those who Trust in Him.V33 it is God who girds me with strength and makes my way perfect.

God speaks back to us; God loves us to speak with Him.

God teaches us to know His voice, to be obedient to His voice. *Proverbs 1: 20, talks about the wisdom crying out in the opening of the Gate.*

Proverbs 2:9 says - then you will understand righteousness and judgment and equity every good path. Today we have the gate of the Lord. The gate of wisdom, we have the righteous gate. V10, when wisdom comes into your heart and knowledge is pleasant to your soul:

When we read God's word, we find ourselves coming closer to God through His words. When we bow our knees before Him and give thanks to Him and worship Him.

Judges 5:8 says that they chose new Gods. Then there was war in the gates. Was there a shield or spear seen among forty thousand in Israel? If we walk away from God, (back slide) and choose the things of this world then we have troubles in our lives and things go wrong. So we must keep in the teaching of God's word, then we will be people of God's word, and we will walk with God in His gates.

Psalm18:21 The Lord rewarded me according to my righteousness: according to the cleanness of my hands as he repaid me. So Righteousness is the gate of the Lord so we must choose God as our God. No other God but the one true God, Creator God.

In the prayer room one evening at 8.30 pm, one of the prayer partners was praying. The man felt the spirit was on him. As the spirit held him, he was swaying to and fro the movement was peaceful as if he was in a current of water (a stream). Then the man got a picture of stones different sizes, perfectly round and so smooth. The spirit said as the stones are moved by the tide and water the current moves and shapes them taking all the rough edges off them. Were the three in the prayer room being shaped by the Trinity (God, Jesus, and the Holy Spirit)?

A few minutes later the man got another picture, this time he was in a large banquet hall with hundreds (could have been thousands) in the hall dancing men/women with more people on the balconies looking down on the dancers. It was as if he was hovering over the top of them, with other people higher than him. There were lots of large beautiful shining chandeliers hanging from the ceiling. At the end of the hall was a brightness so bright and glowing, he was so sure it was God. Then God through the spirit said, "see the dancers moving to the music's rhythm?" (but I couldn't see a band playing).

He felt God was saying *"listen to my rhythm, move to my rhythm, keep in step with Him"* (God) This was what God had said before when He spoken about listening to the rhythm of the falling rain. We must continue to listen for God's voice as He (God) takes us through the Gates

Gate Twenty-Two

Today the man is reading about Nehemiah

He was the kings cup bearer, a man of God, the God of heaven, the God of Israel. Now the enemy had destroyed the Gates of Jerusalem about eleven of them in all, the gates were burnt with fire. In our life there are people that will try and destroy the Gates in our life so we must gear them from the enemy, by following God's commandments, statutes, and judgments, *Nehemiah 1:7*.

So we will have people come into our lives who will try and stop us (turn us away from the God of heaven, the God of creation) they will try and break down the gates of God in you *so be strong and of good courage, do not be troubled, do not be dismayed for the Lord your God is with you wherever you go. Joshua 1:9, 1Peter 4: 1-6, (then read on more of 1Peter 4).*

This particular morning the man was listening to what God had to say to him. God was saying the clay the potter has on the potter's wheel is just a heap of mud till the potter works on it to create something. The wood turner only has a piece of a tree on the lathe, a block of wood till the turner puts the cutting tool to it and creates something. The dressmaker only has a piece of cloth till he or she starts to cut and sews it together.

God said, "when I took a handful of the earth it was just dust of the earth but I moulded it into MAN and gave it life". "Then I took a rib bone from the man which was just a bone but I formed it into Woman", as man and woman are living walking things we are nothing till God moulds us into that wonderful living thing that He (God) wants us to be.

When we give ourselves to Him, to take us through the number of gates that He (God) has for us. (Sorry to say we don't know how many gates there will be and what number we are at?) Just be as in Joshua 1:9.

Eleven gates of Jerusalem Nehemiah 3: God is building up the walls and gates of Jerusalem, God is a mighty God who can build up or pull down. He can build up our gates, and He can pull down or shut the gates as in our lives the different gates have different meanings, the different gates in Jerusalem are for different purposes, as for the gates in our lives.

The gates God has for us is not for our glory but for His glory. He (God) is the all-powerful, nothing is impossible for God. *As we read in Nehemiah 3: that God gave the strength, power, and protection, as they built the walls and gates, for Jerusalem is Gods city.* As with us, we belong to God for his spirit is built in us for God is the righteous gate. He is the main gate of our lives He is the seed gate. Planted in our fathers we are the seed of God. Who lives and dies for Him. Our spirit comes from Him and returns to Him Jesus was God's son, (God's seed).

He lived and died for us, Jesus the seed fell to the earth, and died to live a new. As seeds from the plant falls to the earth it dies but lives to be a new plant and spreads new seeds. We plant seeds into others, through the gates that God takes us through. AMEN.

Reading 1 Samuel 2: 12.

Eli's sons did not know the Lord, (the foot note to this says), (the Hebrew construction speaks of intimately knowing the Lord, being in a relationship with Him, God.) The Psalmist had a very good relationship with God, as they talked to God they worshiped Him. They were in the worship Gate of God.

Nehemiah 12: 27-31. We read, when the walls of Jerusalem were rebuilt the priests followed by the people walked the walls over the gates in praise and worship over the Ephraim Gate, Old Gate, Fish Gate, Sheep Gate, and continued on giving thanks.

Do we stop and give thanks, praise, and worship to our God, when He our God provides all things for us?

Our God provided a time for the man and his wife to walk these very same walls, some months after God had woken the man from his sleep, to write The Gate, (this book). God started to tell him about hinges, Gate hinges, and rusty hinges, God said to him, "what happens when hinges rust"? Being a builder he said to God he would fix them with CRC. "God then said my people have problems and need CRC, "then he said CRC"? "God answered yes (Christ Resurrection Care)".

The word says that Jesus is the way, the truth and the life, we must have that intimate relationship with the Trinity, Father, Son, and Spirit. To be in communication with God every second, minute, hour, day, month, and year. To read every word of the Bible, every page listening for God's voice or a picture in your mind. Jesus said to worship the Father, with all your Mind, Soul, Strength, Heart, Spirit, and Truth.

The devil in Luke 4: 8, when testing Jesus, "Jesus said you will worship the Lord your God and you will serve only Him".

Then Jesus (Y'SHUA) returned to Galilee in the Power of the Spirit. Are you in the power of the Spirit? then don't let the devil test you. Luke 4:14

Samuel 7: 1 when the enemy comes against you. The Philistines were at war with Israel, and they were afraid 7b, V3 Samuel said to all of Israel, to return to the Lord, he also said prepare your hearts for the Lord and serve Him only. He will deliver you out of the hands of the Philistines.

This is the only gate, that God can shut and lock. 7: 8 and all the children of Israel said to Samuel, Do Not Stop Crying To The Lord Our God For Us. God does not want one man to pray. Samuel said return to the Lord God for He wants us all to worship Him and to have Integrity with Him. Samuel did cry out to the Lord and the Lord heard him 7: 9b.

Psalm 145:16, you open your hand and satisfy the desires of every living thing.

God opens His hand and gives us all that we need (the power of the Holy Spirit) He will also hear your cry.

1 Chronicles 5:25 and the children of God acted faithlessly against the God of their fathers, and went ASTRAY, after the Gods of the people of that land. We read this all the time that Gods people are going after other Gods.

We know that we must walk with God, this is still happening to this day that people just do not want God and we know that God gives us all we need daily.

Revelations 4: 1, (Heavenly worship) (John) the first voices I heard speaking with me was like a shofar saying. you must come up here.

Has God spoke to you? Has he said come to me, will you be afraid to go, or will you say YES I am Hear Lord. Will you return to the Lord God, will you go in the spirit to the Lord your God, will you cry out for others, will you be like Samuel and cry out?

Yes, we can come before God, and not be afraid of Him as He loves us so much.

As the man was reading God's word he was thinking of God. In his prayers and again pictures of horses came in to the man's mind, the first one was black, it looked so majestic a wonderful looking horse, then a light brown one with black mixed in and others with black around the eyes. There was even white horses which looked so beautiful. They were all running together as if they were coming to serve God and be selected by the Master God to be first in line. The Bible tell us the first will be last and the last will be first. When the man first came to God he wanted to be first at the gates of heaven.

One-time God gave him a picture of a hill in the dark night. As he looked at the hill a door opened, the door was not in a home it was in the hill. As it opened the light glowed out and there was a silhouette of a man standing there. Now, as the man is older was God opening the gate of a new time in his life, a new path to go down?

The Prayer room.

As he was giving thanks to God and worshipping the Trinity, he was singing in the spirit, as he sang a presence came over him. He got a picture of angels over the prayer room, but one stood out so clear. As the angel was bowing down on one knee he stopped singing for a minute or two then later continued to sing in the spirit again. A wonderful presence came over him like waves of the wind blowing. Then it was like he was dancing but only with his arms, he was walking on air, it was as if he was covering the congregation with the spirit, as his arms came up it was if he was gathering up more of the spirit and flinging it across the room.

Again he got another picture of a big tree and it was so white like polished silver, then the voice said *"yes it's the tree of life the one Eve picked the fruit and gave to Adam,"* the tree which God said not to eat the fruit from. But Eve was conned into eating it. Then God explained about the

89

waves of the spirit, *He said that's my rhythm. The rhythm I want my people to be in, it's a wonderful rhythm, this could be the rhythm gate the presence of the Trinity.* He was asking for more of Him (God the Trinity) and less of me.

The rhythm was like peace, joy, love and healing just like the Trinity has three in one. He then asked God how he could pass this on to others.

He then asked God that whatever He (God) wanted to do through him to go ahead and use him so many others will know Gods rhythm.

Is the power of the spirit in his arms to pass it on, is that what God wanted of him?

The waves of the spirit are like the waves of the sea, pounding onto the rocks as the sea goes up like a wall of white water and recedes back but continues to try and get further each time We must be like the waves and get closer and closer to the Trinity, to God Himself. Are we up to it? yes Lord.

Revelations 22:1-3 This is the last chapter in the Bible.

Then the angel showed me a river of water of life, Torah, bright as crystal going out from the throne of God and the Lamb. In the middle of its street, also on each side of the river, is a tree of life making twelve fruit, yielding its first each month, and the leaves of the tree are used for the healing of the multitudes.

(In my Bible it says in a foot note that people healed of polio which struck people years ago, were healed but were left with scares, the leaves will remove the scares).

Revelations 22: v12, behold I am coming quickly and my reward is with me.

V14 blessed are these who are washing their robes. So that He will give them permission to use the tree of life, and they could enter the gates of the city.

Genesis 2:9 also the tree of life in the midst of the garden, and the tree of knowledge of good and bad, and a river out of Eden to water the garden (Water of life)

Rev V14 goes on to say they could enter the gates of the city (the city of our God).

Rev V17 and the spirit and the bride are saying, 'you must come.' and I the one who hears now say, 'You must come.' And the one who thirsts must come faithfully, the one who wants must now take the water of life as a free gift. Looking back to 22:1 saying the river of water of life, (it has in my Bible the Torah (teaching) so we have the teaching of God, The Bible.

The water of life. If you thirst. "You must come".

The tree of life. If you are sick. "You must come".

God has got all these good things for us, but, "WE MUST COME TO HIM". All through the Bible God our Creator is saying "Come to Me". We must keep ourselves clean for He is with us every second, minute, hour, day, week, month and year. When we are His for ever and ever more let us enjoy the gates God takes us through, and thank Him for the gates He shuts. He truly loves us so very much, we have a Father, Son, and Spirit, the three in one. How Mighty.

Gate Twenty-Three

In the prayer room one evening, he was giving thanks to God, Jesus and Holy Spirit. This night the man was alone and was given a picture of a little girl dancing and singing joyfully, around her was butterflies but when he looked closer they were angels dancing with her, she was so happy. The man had heard earlier that a friend's daughter had not been sleeping very well. On close observation the parents noticed it had all started after a sleep over at a friend's house. The man had been upholding this young girl in his prayer time.

This particular evening the spirit said to him that an evil spirit had latched on to her from the house she had the sleep over in. He was praying for her and the spirit said to him, "that he should tell the girl what he had seen in the picture and that he had to hold the mother's hand and the young girls hand. As the man would be doing this, the evil spirit that he had been praying against would be cast out. The Lord told him, "by doing it this way it would not frighten the young girl".

Matthew 10:27 and what you are hearing in your ear you must immediately proclaim on your roofs.

So this was done on the Sunday after the service (15-3-2015).

The man was by himself one day and asked God about some of the sick people and why they had not been healed. He was asking about the right Keys to the sickness gate, the right prayer to their healing, because we have prayed many times for some of the people and no healing has taken place. God was saying *that it was not a steel key* (what do you mean God, "not a steel key?").

The man was thinking of a locked gate key? *"NO, NO it's a music key, (when we sing in the key of")*, this took me back to God's rhythm as when we are in rhythm with God we are in the right key, so we move with God and for God. If we sing in the wrong key it does not sound right, so as in *Matthew 10: 27, we must hear in our EAR.*

92

So when we are praying or singing we must listen for His voice and stay in rhythm with God.

Matthew 10: 20 For it will not be those speaking, but it will be the spirit of your Father the one who speaks through you Amen, Amen let it be Lord.

Psalm 23: King David always knew that God was with him, and how God provided all things for him. David was always giving thanks to God, and God guided him on the right path through the right gates. God made his cup run over with blessings, and with the spirit of God. Is your cup running over with the Holy Spirit? So we can dwell in the house of the Lord forever.

Jesus said in Matthew 11: 27 That Jesus wants to reveal the Father to us, V 28 says, come to me all you who are weary and are burdened, and I will give you rest.

Jesus wants to put us on the right path, through the right gate, Matt V25. Even Jesus (Y'SHUA) is praising God, the Father of heaven and earth and of all life.

Matt V29 Jesus is saying, learn from Him, for He is gentle and humble in heart, for if we do this we will find rest in our lives, so we must come to God, Jesus and the Holy Spirit, are you there yet?

The man was in a prayer time with one of the group, as he was praying a picture came to him of a person in deep water. This person was panicking and fearful of the deep water. It looked like the person could not find their way out of the water and was very distressed. The man did not know the person as he could not see their face and did not know whether it was male or female, but knew that he had to pray for this person. When Stewart, one of his prayer partners had finished his pray the man informed him about the picture and prayed that God would help the person by sending an angel to lift this person from the deep water.

The man believes that this is the intercessory prayer gate that God has opened to them so he could be obedient to God and pray for others like this person in the water. The next day the man was with another prayer partner Ken, in their prayer time God gave the man another picture of a flame. He asked God about this and God said *"it's the Holy Spirit"*, *it is like the perpetual light that is in many churches around the world, the same light that Moses had to place in the Tent.* In those days it was an oil lamp so it was a flame which would never go out. (The priests would fill them with oil every day).

God was saying to him that the flame of the spirit (Holy Spirit) (God's Spirit) was in Ken and him, and would never be put out, no one in this world can put it out, God has placed it in them for His work on earth that God has for them.

So with the flame of the spirit in us we can come closer and closer to God and Jesus, we should not be fearful for God said *"fear not for I am with you"*. So God is the great I AM.

I give thanks to God for his word. I praise Him. Amen.

11 Chronicles 23: 20 here it talks about the High Gate, it says: And they come through the High gate into the Kings house, and set the King upon the Throne of the Kingdom.

In Matthew 19: 23 Jesus is telling his disciples that it is difficult for a rich person to enter the Kingdom of the heaven, the bible tells us that the Gate is narrow to the Kingdom and that it is the only gate into the Kingdom.

The man is talking and praying to the Lord, always giving thanks and praise for all He has done for us all. God was saying that His word (the Bible), His teaching is all from Him. It's a key to each lock on the gate so every gate we come to that is locked it's in his word (the Torah Teaching), every word is a key to our gates of life. So in reading the bible we get the key to God's Kingdom!! And God's will for us.

No matter which gate we are at in our lives, God is the Gate man. Ready to talk us through the right gate, the word (Bible) says trust in the Lord always. Most times that is very hard for us to do especially if we are going through a rough time. Stay in touch with God, Jesus, and the Holy Spirit. The Trinity is not just a word, it is life.

Let us live it as God wants us to. Are you healthy, wealthy, and wise?

God's word THE BIBLE,

John 3: 16 God so loved the world that he gave his only Son, that whoever believed in Him will have eternal life. AMEN.

Another picture the man got one day was of a fox and the chicken shed. The fox was going around and around the shed looking for an opening to get to the chickens in side. God said to him that *the fox was Satan*, and that he was around looking for people to join the powers of darkness.

Then the man got another picture of thick fog, and in the thick fog was a big sailing ship. This old sailing ship was a very dark image in the fog, then God said *the old fox is Satan, the shed and the ship being the church. He prayed for the leadership, the selection team and the church* for the fog to be cleared, and that we would have clearer views as God steered the ship. Then God took him back to the Sunday when he got a picture of the big angel covering the church. It is so easy to lock ourselves away in our homes. And it is so easy to get lost in the fog.

Mark 4: Y'SHUA (Jesus) had chosen the twelve disciples, and as always Jesus was teaching them the word of God. When we have the Holy Spirit within us the Spirit teaches us the same way. As Jesus was teaching and telling them about the sower many times He was saying "He who has ears to hear must continually listen" Mark 4: 9.

When we are in prayer with God we must listen, and see with our hearts pictures. God will tell us the meanings of them, and we will learn how to listen to Him (God). Then we will come to know the Master's voice, like the seed of the Savior and proclaim His word.

Mark 4:40 Jesus said to them after calming the storm, "why are you timid, do you not have faith?" When God takes us through the listening gate. He will take us through the bold gate so we can be bold and strong for Him. He will use us to speak out for Him, and it will be in His time.

The man was talking to Ken about the two pictures God had given to him about the fox and the ship. Ken gave an explanation of where he felt these pictures were from.

Song of Songs 2: 15 it says, take us the foxes, the little foxes that spoil the vines, for our vines have tender grapes. The foxes as being Satan, the small foxes

95

being his followers. God is the vine we are the branches, the tender grapes are what the fox comes to spoil, the vines tender grapes, so God gave the man the warning to pray for the congregation against the evil ones. (Y'SHUA) Jesus wants us to keep on praying always.

We must continually pray for the people and against the vine getting spoiled. Amen.

Genesis 7: 1 God said to Noah, Come into the box. (Boat the ARK).

God was already inside telling Noah to Come.

God always asks us to come to him, and it is up to us whether we go to Him or not. God longs for us to come to Him, its only when we have problems do we go to Him. When things are going OK we stay away from God. People think when they have read the bible that's it, but God wants us to read it all the time, when we are reading God's word He is with us and says COME,

God said to Noah, "make a box", maybe Noah thought a small box but God's box was 450 feet long, 75 feet wide and 45 feet high. Most men would say 'what and for all the animals as well!' but Noah took on the job God had given him. Because Noah walked and talked to God, Noah worshiped God just like Noah's great, great, great Father Enoch did in,

Genesis 5: 21 say Enoch walked with God v24 says that Enoch was three hundred and sixty-five years old (365 years old) and God took him. This sounds like God took him straight to heaven, well it tells us that he did not die on earth. We read that this was no small job for Noah, people were talking about him, they were saying he was mad because they were miles from the ocean and this was not the thing to do in building a large boat. The rains came and lifted the boat up and they were on the water for quite long time. Noah lived to be nine hundred and fifty years old (950 years) the bible does not say that he died (Did God Take Him Like Enoch?) Has God given you a job. When God gives us a picture or a message do we leave it? or deliver it?

The man was talking to Ken one evening about when we get mail delivered by the postman it has the address on the envelope. He felt God say we are like the mail room and the one to deliver the letters.

When God gives us a picture or a word we have to sort it out and get the right address, and the right time to deliver it. The man was saying when he had been overseas in different churches God had given him a word for healing or a person who needed to come to the Lord for prayer. One time he was on a tour when God said to him that he should sing a song of thanks giving. He obeyed God and did this. We must always be ready to be alert to God's voice and His timing.

Being alert to God through the Spirit, God teaches us to listen and to know His voice, (do not worry this could take years but it will happen when God wants you He will talk to you). The man and one of the prayer partners Stewart were in the prayer room when God gave him a picture of an igloo. Igloos are made of ice blocks, but this one was concrete blocks with a big hole in it. He asked God what the meaning of this was and God said, *"the evil one is loose"*. So at all times and I mean all times, we have to be on guard like the gate keepers of old. (alert to his lies that the evil one says to us). Satan will do all he can to turn us away from the Trinity, The Father, The Son, and The Spirit.

Here in Genesis 24: 60 we read that God said to Rebeccah that she would be the mother of thousands of myriads, and let your seed possess the gate of those who hate them. That we can control the gates of the people, that hate us through being with God.

In Genesis 28: 16-17 Jacobs ladder. Jacob awakened from sleep, and said how awesome is this place, this is none other but the house of God, and this is the gate of heaven, the ladder set upon the earth and reaching to heaven. With the angels going up and down, God gave Jacob the picture of this thousands of years ago. But God still gives His people the pictures today, we still go through some of the same Gates.

In my reading today in *Mark 7: 16 again we read in V16 if someone has ears to hear he must now listen. We must always be listening for God's voice,* we hear the birds and the sound of water.

Do We Block Out God?

God longs for us to listen to Him. God longs for us to speak with Him. God longs for us to be obedient to what He says. The most important thing is to spend time with God. Praying, worship and reading God's word each day. Time with Him (God) is like money in the bank it multiples, but you get more and more out of God than you will ever get out of the bank.

Gate Twenty-Four

Reading Genesis 37: 5 we read about Joseph's dream or pictures, God was with Joseph and was taking Joseph through the Gate. Joseph told his brothers and father about the dream and they didn't know what the dream was about. Later Joseph's brothers sold him to the traders (God was with him) so this took Joseph through another gate, this gate was for God's purpose.

When we look at Exodus 4:10 Moses was reluctant to go through the gate that God wanted him to go through. God says in V15 "And you will speak to him and put words in his mouth, and I AM will be with your mouth and with his mouth, and will teach you what you will do". (the mouth of Moses and Aaron).

God is in our mouth as we speak out for Him (God) to others or in the congregation where we fellowship. V12 says, "now go I AM, will be with your mouth, and I will teach you what you will say", we must go through the gate God has for us which will work for God's kingdom and His glory.

Our prayer for healing

Many times we pray for healing, how do we pray? With our heartfelt prayers to God are we the gate to healing when we ask God (God is the healer)? If we open our prayer gate to God to come through us to the person we are praying for, as we touch the person and through the Holy Spirit which is in us, then, if this is God's will He will heal through our gate. We are not the healer but the connection for God to that person so He (God) can heal them.

So we, like Moses are the go between the "wifi" if you like, the "net" Jesus said to the disciples *"follow Me and I will make you fishers of men"* (the net). Some time ago God gave the man a picture of a net across a river, the river as being the church, the net was there to stop the people from sailing away downstream, the net was strong with small holes so they would not get through. God is holding the net, for God is our Anchor so when we pray for people for healing our words and our heart has to be right.

In my reading to day. Leviticus 26: 23-26 "God is saying that if we don't walk with Him, we walk contrary to Him then God will walk contrary to us". The end of V25 "I shall send the pestilence among you and you will be delivered into the hands of the enemy". God will break us but will bring us back to Himself (God.)

God talked about the bread, the bread ten women will bake in one oven and they will deliver to you your bread again by weight, and you will eat and not be satisfied. God (the bread) will come back and walk with us and we will want more and more of God. V42 "then I shall remember my covenant with Jacob, Isaac, and Abraham".

For God is the HEALER

The man recalls reading God's word in Numbers a book in the Bible. As he was reading he felt that God was saying that there are many gates in our lives. Reading about Israel, God tried to keep them on the right path and through the right gate.

If we go through the wrong gate we get locked in to that path and we try to go back to get out of that situation, but the gate is locked, and it takes us a long time to get back to the right path again.

God says "if we follow his instructions and we do the right thing then our life will go well, till we get to the next gate". The bible tells us that to get into heaven we have to go through the (narrow gate) for this is the gate we must go through.

In life there are many choices we make, so we need to make the right choices. Follow the spirit of God and the right gate will stand out. As we read in Numbers, Moses was the shepherd, he was the one through God to take the Israelites through the right gate.

Today we have the Holy Spirit to take us through the right gate, some churches today do not want to follow the Holy Spirit they want to follow other churches just like Israel, they followed the other people into worshiping the wrong God.

What Does God Require, Deuteronomy 10: 20
You will revere the Lord your God.
You will serve Him and you will cleave to Him.
And swear by His name.

Cleaver to Him as God said to him, "stick to Him". The man was unsure what this meant so asked God for the meaning. God said, "when you use glue to put things together you put glue on both sides, *when it dries it remains stuck together*".

When you bring them together it sticks fast *"(cleaver to me), stick to me like glue"*. God wants us to worship him, only him and cleaver to Him.

Deuteronomy 11:1 there you will always love the Lord your God and keep His Ordinances.

And all that is in you cleaver to Gods word (His every word) and worship Him with all your being (every part of you).

1 Samuel 1:9 When Hannah gave birth to Samuel it was a gift from God, and she gave him back to God. It took Samuel four times to know God's voice, four times God called him, we need to know God's voice. 1 Samuel 3: 1-10 We need to know when the Spirit of God is on us, we need to cleaver to God (Stick like glue to God) so when we walk, God walks with us and we with Him, The Great I Am.

The Gate into God's Present.

As God teaches us through His spirit, The Holy Spirit the true communicator, with God the spirit that opens the gate.

The man recalls one morning in church as the congregation was singing the last song there had been a call from the pastor for anyone who needed prayer to come forward.

There was a young couple with two very young children who went up for prayer and three ladies went up to pray for them. As the man was singing the Lord gave him a picture of the couple with a gold and silver chain around them. God said go and pray for them and tell them about the chains. (he said to God, what, are you sure?)

So at the end of the song he went up to the young couple and the ladies who were praying for them and touched them. God gave him the words to pray, the other ladies were about to leave but he called them back.

God was telling them through him that the chain of gold and silver was of power, healing and love. God's protection that no one or anything can break God's chain.

Then he was just about to finish when the child that the mother was holding lifted its hand up and touched his face with its little hand. WOW!! WOW!! he believed that this was God's Spirit touching him. He said it was like the spirit was saying thank you to him. Then he opened his eyes and the baby was still touching his face and was wanting to kiss him. The look that the baby gave to him was as if to say thank you, he kissed the baby as tears were starting to fill his eyes. WOW!! what a blessing he received for being obedient that day. So the spirit of God opened the gate into God's presents, so we never know how God will touch us when you know the gate is open go through. The Obedient Gate.

Gate Twenty-Five

The man was taken with another picture, as he was sitting in church listening to the pastor preach, God showed him a picture of a hand. As he watched the hand, a torch came into the picture and moved into the hand. The hand started to move, then God through the spirit *"said this is the flame of the spirit to light or ignite the spirit of others"*. Then *"God told him to walk around the church singing in the spirit to the congregation so the people could reach out and take the flame (to enlighten their spirits)"*.

He was sitting there saying to God, when, how, what, and what song? And 'Oh no are you speaking to me God?' Then he was at the gate God had opened for him to go through. *'God said go'*, the pastor was praying so he waited, then told the people about the picture, and what God wanted him to do. All the time he was thinking what would he sing, how would he start? he started to walk then the spirit of God took over his mouth (mouth gate) it opened and a powerful song in the spirit came out. Then he felt as if he had been lifted up and his feet were wheels, he seemed to be floating around the church.

After the last song a lady came to him and said she could not understand the song but she got a picture. She said "when you started to sing a picture came to her of a mountain with the sun just rising. God said to her, look up at the bright sun, there was other people in the picture but they had their backs to the sun. As the sun started to rise over the mountain people turned and looked to the sun, as the valley became lighter all the people were looking to the sun. All this happened as you were moving around the church and as you stopped singing that was when the valley was in full sun".

(Jesus is the light of the world) is the spirit preparing us for the coming of the Lord Jesus (Y'SHUA) our Messiah our Lord and Savior of our Souls, the Redeemer. AMEN.

Isaiah 55: 3

Incline your ear and come to me Listen! Obey and your inner being will LIVE! I will cut an everlasting covenant with you. God says if we listen to His voice.

We must discern God's voice, discernment in our spirits and obey his leading. This is another gate God takes us through.

Jeremiah 17: 24

And it will be if you Diligently Listen to me says the Lord. When we listen to the voice of God on Obedience. When we walk with God. When we cleaver to God (stick to him).

When we glue things together it's hard to get them apart, so should we stick to God? Being as one not coming apart, to be in the listening Gate.

An evening service 8.15 pm. The picture gate.

This night in the worship time God gave him a picture of a horse (just the head). It was as if he was looking from above, looking at the neck and mane of the horse. It was a white horse. Then he heard God say, *"there are people sitting on horses, they need to hold onto the mane if they want to serve God for they will be going swiftly so they need to hang on"*. There have been times that God has taken him in the spirit and soared with Him in the clouds and this sure feels pretty fast.

Amos 5: 14-15
Seek good and not bad! So you can live and so the Lord God of hosts will be with you as you have spoken. V15, Hate evil! Love good! Establish justice in the Gate!

God of hosts will be gracious to the remnant of Joseph.

The gate of goodness is where we should be. Do not go into the gate of badness (Evil), stay in the gate of good and God will always be with you. Listen to God's voice, walk with him, talk with him and stay in God's word. THE GATE OF LIFE.

The Gate of Disobedience or gate of Obedience.

Let's look at Jonah, God gave Jonah the task to go to Nineveh but Jonah went the other way and trouble struck the ship in high seas. The sailors cast Jonah into the sea, he went down to the bottom of the sea, this was his lowest part (was this his death NO!! God sent a big fish and he was swallowed up inside for three days,)

Jonah prayed to God and talked to God for three days, the fish must have travelled miles. Did God send the fish towards Nineveh?

The fish vomited Jonah out on dry land v 2:11. And God spoke to Jonah again "Go to Nineveh", God was opening the gate again for Jonah. V 3:1 (the foot note for 2:7 the gate of the underworld). Was this Jonah's last gate death?

The Trouble gate

Haggai 2: 17
The Lord is telling us. V17 I struck you with blight, mildew and hail in all your labors. (troubles) of your hands. and God said "yet you did not turn to me". When we go through this gate we try to get out in our own power and not turn to God. We go through the wrong gate.

Zechariah 1: 3
'return to me says the Lord of Hosts, then I shall turn to you says the Lord'

We must turn from the evil ways and our evil doings and turn to Him the Lord of hosts.

Zechariah 8: 16
(Do these things) these are the things that you will do, everybody speak the truth to your neighbor, execute the judgment of truth and peace in your gates, (your life).

"Do not devise evil in your hearts against his neighbor, and do not love any false oath for all these things are things that I HATE" SAYS THE LORD.

In the gates of our life the word of God the Torah (Teaching of God) The Bible. God talks to us today just as He talked to the prophets of old, we just have to listen for His voice.

Open the ear gate, read God's word, the Bible, the Torah, these are God's teachings. Walk and talk with Him, and God will take us through the right gate. Have that right peace and truth in your gates. God is always with us and His spirit is within us Amen.

Psalm 9: 14 the Death gate

In the Psalms we read 'you who lift me up from the gates of death', these are the death gates so there is more than one death gate. Jonah thought he was at the death gate but NO, God lifted him up from the death gate, it wasn't his time. V15 "so I can tell of all your praise in the gates of the daughter of Zion. I will rejoice exuberantly in your deliverance!"

So we are involved with other people's gates. We must go through lots of gates in a life time.

Psalm 24: 7
Lift up your heads, O you gates and be lifted up, you everlasting doors, and the King of Glory will come in. V8 Who is the King of Glory? THE LORD strong and mighty, the LORD mighty in battle.

No matter which gate we are in or going through the King of Glory will lift us up and protect us from the evil one. When we have given our hearts to God, Jesus and the Holy Spirit we go through the gate of Holiness, we give our life back to God so we must always read His word, we must always come to Him.

We must walk with Him, talk with Him, giving thanks always and always praise Him with a grateful heart. To always be in God's gate, be strong, bold, and to trust in the Lord always have God, Jesus and the Holy Spirit first in our life everyday Amen.

Psalm 87:2

We read about God, He loves the gates of Zion.

If we look at this and read it, putting our name in the place of Zion.

Eg. God loves the gates (name) we see that God loves our gates when He (God) takes us through the gates of life.

Our lives each day depending on how long God wants us to be in each gate. It maybe days, weeks, months, years, it's all up to God,

God has us in the palm of His hand, He has all our days numbered right till we go through the heavenly gates and stand before our God, Y'SHUA (Jesus), through the Holy Spirit he will take us.

Psalm 107: 16

No matter which gate we are in, if we feel trapped in darkness and our iniquities God can break the gates of our enemies. God in *V16 'for He has broken the gates of bronze and cut the bars of iron asunder'*.

This is telling us God can do anything, and that God is in our gates no matter which gate we are at or in, for God loves the gates of your life. Call out to your God and always give thanks and God will lift you up and out of the problem you are in, to encourage you read on in *Psalm 107*. See what God can do for you but you must always give thanks and be steadfast in the Trinity. Father God, Jesus the son and the Holy Spirit, walk and talk with them, the Trinity.

Psalm 118 19-20

V19 The gate of righteousness'.

V 20 This is the gate of the Lord.

Into which the righteous will enter to be righteous, we have to change when we are righteous. If we do the right thing and we are made righteous by our faith and also our behavior has to change, then our lives will be turned around.

Being made righteous by faith and the grace of God to become a better person so with faith and consistent to God it brings the gift of righteousness. We can then go through the Gate of Righteousness. The Gate of the Lord.

When we commit our life to God and walk and talk with him (God) the Lord God, He will guide us in our going out and our coming in, this will be for evermore.

Psalm 121: 8

So this is telling us that God takes us through the different gates of our life if we commit ourselves to him, doing the right thing pleases God and being faithful to Him. Walking and talking to our God, listening to

God's voice as we take our walk daily with God. Giving thanks to God for all, YES all, He will do through the different gates.

Proverbs 6: 22-23

When we walk, the commandments, will lead us, when we rest it will keep us, and when we awake it will talk with us, v23 for the commandment is a lamp and the Torah (teaching) is light.

The Bible tells us that *Jesus is the Truth, the Way and the Light (life).*

The commandment God gave us; God must be the commandment.

So the Bible is telling us that God the commandment is with us all the time, so we can walk, sleep and talk to God at any time in the darkness of our life, God will take us through the right Gate for He (God) is the lamp beneath our feet.

He is the light in the reading of the word, the Torah, so we must become a person of the light. Be a light gate.

So when you are reading God's word The Torah (teachings) does God turn on the light for you to understand what you are reading?

Proverbs 17:19 here we read of the mouth gate. Sometimes this Gate lets us down. When opened it can love, for it will build up or it can knock down. It can open up joy or it can hurt. It can bring encouragement to others and it can part friends from the overflow from our hearts it exalts God our Father, Y'SHUA (Jesus) and the Holy Spirit.

When we are in this gate we need to slow down, think of what we say and how to say it so we can build up, (encourage) not knock down, listen to the spirit and what God is saying to you through the spirit. God will open that gate and God will shut that gate. *(18:4 Read this passage)*

When you sense you are within a certain gate, talk to God, ask for the spirit and move in the spirit. God will lead you many times. When you have prayed and given thanks to God the spirit will speak out through you.

In a tongue which you have not learned yourself but in a tongue that God has given you.

God through the spirit may give the man a picture, word to interpret or it may be a tongue.

It may be a song of healing so you will be moving in the spirit, it will be the gate that God wants you in at that time. The healing gate, this is allowing God to heal people and to bring people closer to Him (God). God is the Trinity, Father, Son and Spirit. And you will know when they are with you always, AMEN.

Gate Twenty-Six

Talking to God - the Mouth Gate

Thank you Father for all things; you bless us with your abundant love. You set our path through the gates of life, guarding us each day, providing us with what we need and teaching us your ways. And how to listen to your voice and to walk with you. Your word feeds us and sustains us, giving us the strength to walk with you through the gates. Your words give us understanding of how mighty you are, and how great your love is for us.

When we take time to listen to you, and be with you in your word we come to understand you more.

In the man's reading.

Job 38:17 Have the gates of death been opened for you or have you seen the doors of the shadow of death? When God opened the Red Sea for the people of Israel to go through, they went through on dry ground. Usually the sea bed is always wet, but by God's power He dried it up with in minutes. Today as we go through trials and problems, God makes a way through for us, opening the right gate for us, making the path for us and God walks with us all the way.

The Israelites knew it was a dead end for them at the Red Sea with the Egyptians behind them wanting to take them back to Egypt. It was a sink or swim situation, or be killed situation. Moses trusted God, and what God told him to do was lift his staff and his hands above the waters and God opened the gate. So when we walk and talk to God He opens the gate. When we read in the New Testament about Jesus and how he took over the opening of the gates, Jesus opened many gates, the eye gate, the mouth gate, the ear gate, the life gate and it goes on and on. The Bible tells us that Jesus is the way, the truth and the life AMEN.

There are many gates in the kingdom of Heaven, and there are many rooms in the house of God. *Luke 13: 22-30 v24 Jesus is saying that we must enter through the narrow door, and some say through the narrow Gate, Jesus is saying all through his teachings how we must live.*

Jesus tells us, *"it's going to be hard to enter the kingdom of heaven".*

Jesus is saying in Luke 13:6 *"if there is no fruit on the tree cut it out".* We must bear fruit in our lives, fruit for the kingdom, we must not be barren trees.

Luke 13: 25

When the Master shuts the gate He will not open it unless He knows the one standing at the gate. This is going to be very hard for some people. We must walk with him and talk with him, we must spend the time with him then He (God, Jesus, and Holy Spirit) will know our voice. Then maybe, God or Jesus will open the gate to the kingdom, (the house of God).

We must do the right thing, we must tie ourselves to God to be in rhythm with Him (like being tied to someone in a three legged race, we must keep in rhythm with that person to win), then we go through the winner's gate.

In *Deuteronomy* God talks about the gates He will give us.

It is God who takes us into the different gates, He leads us and puts us where He wants us to be for his purpose, it is always God's ways not our ways. God opens and closes the gates.

In *Lamentations 2:9* God is saying about the gates of the land, but also shows us and tells us about the gates in our lives, and about God's Bible, the Torah (teaching). God can break the locks on our gates.

(V 2:9 It says our gates have sunk into the ground).

(doubting, depression, and oppression). Three gates that we come to we see today in the Bible, is no more in the homes, schools, and lives of lots of people today.

Philippians 2:5 To shine our light in the world when we become of the Lord Y'SHUA (Jesus). We should shine our light like the stars in the night sky. We as believers should shine in this dark world, we are to be light to others (none believers) till Y'SHUA (Jesus) returns for us all.

26/6/2016 Its a Sunday morning, the worship pastor Luke was preaching. God gave the man a picture of alabaster jars, big jars, God said to the man, *"do you see them, do you know the story where Jesus was at the wedding?"* The man replied "yes, I have read this". God said *"it's time for some people to dip their cups into the jars so that He (God) can take them into the promised land".*

God wanted the man to take this to the people in the congregation to encourage them to come to Him, to walk and talk with Him, but first they must take the first step towards Him. God knows the ones that He wants to come to Him, God in His word says, he who has ears listen, he who has eyes open them and look.

The ear Gate.

The Spirit Gate.

John 2:1-12 The wedding at Cana.

When we dip our cup into the jar we allow God to do work in our lives, in the jar are good things like healing, love, peace and hope. God wants to take us into Himself. The wine at the wedding was the best wine, that's what God was saying. God wants the best for us, the very best, but if we do not dip into God's jar we will not get the best.

There is one good thing about the jars, they are big and we can continue to dip our cups into it and get the goodness that God has for us. The jars and wine are God's love, so by coming to God each and every day we can dip into the jars of God's goodness, the Word. AMEN.

When I came before the Lord God in prayer I was taken in the spirit to Moses Law's. Moses was not a well-educated man. God wrote the laws and commandments on stone tablets then Moses took them to the people. They are talked about (in the bible) as Moses laws, but they were God's Laws. I was thinking of this book 'The Gate' which God had told me to write, I felt I could relate to Moses, not being well educated, so it is God who writes this book. I may hold the pen but God is the writer.

Just like the Bible, its God's word but many people will hold the pen, and God will give them the words. The Gate is God's word placed together to encourage His people to walk and talk with Him (God).

God knows everyone, and opens each and every gate in our lives because He (God) is the A and Z the Beginning and the End. Enjoy the path through each gate as God says, come to Me. AMEN.

Moses and Joshua at the gate of the promise land, God opened the gate for Joshua BUT closed the gate to Moses. We must be right with God all the time otherwise we will miss the gate, it will close and remain shut.

In James 4:8 it says 'draw near to God and He (God) will draw near to you'.

I was in the last book of the bible, *Revelations 21: v12-15*

We read that the writer is seeing the new Jerusalem, the new city descending from heaven, the writer tells us that the city has high walls and Twelve Gates. Three on the east, three north, three south, and three west. At the start of getting these writings from God regarding this book 'The Gate', it was in my readings the following day about the East Gate being shut. There in *Revelations 21:15 it tells us that the Gates of the new Jerusalem will never be SHUT.*

Also the twelve gates are made of pearls, and the streets are pure gold. They say that the last gate we enter are the 'Pearly Gates', this sounds like the gates of the new Jerusalem and the streets paved in gold.

What a wonderful place to be after going through the gates of life with God, Jesus, and the Holy Spirit, the three in one (wow!! The three Gates of the East wall). I am so blessed that God has shown me that the best gates are God, Jesus, and Holy Spirit, that they are the three East Gates.

These gates maybe the last gates the bible talks about but while we walk on this earth for God there will be more gates that God will take us through for His Kingdom.   AMEN to that.

Gate Twenty-Seven

Sunday morning in church, the Lord gave the man a picture of a woman and the back of a man (He thought it was him). The man was holding flames of fire in his hands, and the Spirit was saying to give some of the fire to others who would like it (this was the spirit of God). Was God opening the gate of the Holy Spirit for others to take?

As he was thinking of what and how to do this, he started to move to the front of the church, he approached the pastor and was given permission to talk to the congregation. At the end of the service approximately eight couples came to him for prayer and the fire of the Holy Spirit.

The Spirit is pleased with us when we move in obedience to His will.

On the 27/9/2016 in his pray time, God was saying to him about circumcision. *God was saying that we must circumcise our hearts to the Lord (to give our hearts to the Lord).* This is for men and woman to take away the foreskins of our hearts, removing the barriers of our hearts.

Paul wrote in Galatians 5:2 referring to this, *by taking away all the things of the world from out of the heart, and become circumcised to God.* This is for all men and women.

It is important to be close to our God, to walk and talk with Him so we can destroy the walls we put up against the Lord our God.

As he worshipped the Lord our God in one of the Sunday evening prayer meetings the Lord gave him a picture of a gate which was closed with a barb wire fence around it. The spirit said to him that Jesus had opened the gate to the Father but the gate had been shut. The Spirit was saying to him that the barb wire was the fences we build up against God. The church people are building up fences against God, the Son, and Spirit. The prayer time continued and God showed him another picture,

114

this was of a hose clip and the Spirit said to him "tighten it up". He asked again what did this mean? Another person prayed about coming closer to God, so he thought this prayer was part of the picture he had just been given.

He asked others in the group if God was saying to listen and to come closer and closer to Him because as we tighten up the hose clip it comes closer and closer.

In his time with God and reading His word, he was reading in *Psalm 7 & 8* about how King David was always getting closer to God, singing and talking to God. In *v9* David says to God, "judge me" God will judge His people. In *Revelations* it tells us what is going to happen to the world. God is going to shut the gates to heaven to all the followers of the evil one. *Revelations 15* also says we must come closer to God, we must praise God, sing Psalms to Him and bow down to the God of all Gods, AMEN. When Jesus returns.

Psalm 8: King David asks God to be gracious to him, for God is the one who lifts us up from our troubles and from the gates of death of the daughter of Zion.

David was always ready to praise God; he knows that God is always with him. David would speak to God and God answered. God speaks to the man in pictures and a few words, through the Spirit we come closer to God when we have God in our hearts. We take God with us everywhere we go, we walk, run, swim, work, sleep, God is there with us 24/7.

Bonding

Today God in the man's prayer time was saying about bonding men and women to each other and to God. (we are all different).

How a man is so different to a woman that we must bond together which sometimes takes time to bond. You could say it's like taking two different materials and gluing them together.

We have to use the right glue; we have to bond to God.

This takes time and the right glue, the word of God, His teaching and being in prayer with Him.

115

The glue we use today is instant, some takes time to set, some glue reacts straight away on contact. When we place glue on two pieces of material and bring them together it bonds them both together.

The reading today. (the Narrow gate that leads to life) or (the wide gate to destruction).

Noah was bonded to God. King David was bonded to God, Solomon was bonded to God, Matthew also was bonded to God.

Matthew 12: 43 (the unclean spirit)

When we cast out an unclean spirit out of a person, the house of that person becomes clean, but we must lock the gate of that clean house of that person. So the unclean spirit cannot return with seven others spirits. We know the power of the evil spirits but the power of God is much stronger than the evil one. So we lock the gate behind us, and encourage the one with the clean house to keep in the word of God the Father to maintain the clean house and person.

We need to keep in prayer and in the word of God each and every day to keep the evil locked out. As *Y'SHUA, (Jesus) said this is an evil generation we live in so be strong for the Lord your God is with you.*

In the prayer room one evening with his prayer partners they were discussing how great it is to be led by the Lord our God. As they were praying God showed the man a picture of horses, one with a band around its head just below the eyes, another with a nose bag on eating, then a very good looking brown stallion.

Then a fox (Satan), a potter's wheel and a woman in travail. He asked for the woman's name so they could pray for her.

God answered him with the following explanation:

The Woman - *she needed prayer.*

The horse with the nose bag on - *to eat our fill of God's Word.*

The Fox - *trying to steel God's People away.*

The Potter's wheel - *to keep our balances with God so He can mold us.*

116

16/12/16 Once again in the prayer time one evening God spoke to the man and said, *"do not compare yourself to others who God had made"*. The next morning in his reading *Mark 4: 23 Jesus is saying to the disciples, "whoever has ears to hear must listen steadily"* if we did not have ears and listened, we would not hear God speak to them. (Y'SHUA) Jesus through the Bible is teaching us to listen to God and to come to God, to walk and talk to Him the Trinity, Father, Son, and Spirit.

We need to hear every word our Lord God says to us as we may have to pass each word on to others.

MARK: 9: v50 Salt is Good.

But if salt became salt-less how would you season? You have salt in yourselves, yes we are made up of salt in our bones. Our bones are 23% sodium so we must eat the foods that have sodium in them. If we do not have 23% of sodium in our diet then the body pulls the sodium from the bones, thus making them weak.

You must continually live in peace with one another, God is saying that we must season others with the word that is within us. God's word says if salt loses its saltiness then it is no good.

If we do not read and keep God's word within us we will not be able to season others to God.

This also stops the temptations to sin, and with Gods word (the salt) within us we can season others through God's word.

The man was sitting watching the white clouds move across the blue sky one day. And his mind was going back in time and thinking how God moves in our lives as we go from one thing to another. He closed his eyes and thinking what God had done in his life and what God had done in other people's lives he thought about how God whispers to us. Most times we do not hear the whisper of God.

He opened his eyes and was looking out of the window at the garden and wow wow!! The sun was bright, the colors were wonderful, what an awesome sight. The trees soaking up the wonderful warmth of the sun.

At that first moment he thought of heaven, was he there, no he was still sitting in his seat looking at the garden.

He really felt that God was whispering to him saying that after the pain and suffering we endure on earth, we will open our eyes in heaven and see the real beauty there.

He was saying that the peace he felt was so amazing at the time. We read in the bible that the peace that Y'SHUA (Jesus the Messiah) left us was so perfect that the peace is refined seven times more than silver. In the book of *Mark 16:15 He said to them, you must now preach the good news to the whole world, to all creation. V16 The one who believes and is immersed, will be delivered/saved V17 signs and wonders will follow after those who believe in My name they will cast out demons, they will speak in new languages.*

In the book of *Esther 1*: the King was having a banquet and called to have his wife brought in. The King's name was Ahasuerus, his wife's name was Vashti. The King's wife Vashti refused to come to the King when he summoned her to his presence. King sent a message to all the people in his kingdom in their own language that every man should be the ruler of his own home.

Is this where the spirit of domination started in men and their homes.

That night in the prayer room with one of his prayer partners he was praying and God showed him a picture of God himself. The man could only see God side on. From God's mouth he could see vapor, lots of vapor like a roaring wind. As the other person stopped praying he relayed the picture to them, and while he was praising and thanking God, God said *"the vapor was the Holy Spirit"* and God was blowing it all over the world. As he was praying he could feel within him the Spirit as God was filling him up.

After a restless sleep he woke with the whisper of the Spirit in his mind and it was saying about a flower, a large flower. He could see this flower and its colour was red, yellow, and in bud, but it snapped off the stem. He started to think and wondered what this could mean.

The whisper was telling him about how God forms the flower to grow and to be in the protection of the outer leaves till the time is right for it to show its beauty as it pushes through the outer leaves. It then comes to maturity and puts out its fragrance out to the world.

When do we, as God's people come to maturity and put out God's fragrance and colour to show the world around us?

With the wonderful work God has done in our life, are we a strong flower head, or are we like the bud that snapped off before we come to maturity in God? Is the weight of the world and our daily life too hard for us?

Let us put our trust in the gardener God, He will make us strong then we will mature and have God's fragrance in us.

If you would like to read *2 Corinthians 4: 16. on living by faith.*

Gate Twenty-Eight

In church God, was speaking to the man about communion, the Lord's supper, the wine and the bread, about the seed of wheat that falls to the ground to live a new. *John 12:24 that Jesus was the seed that died to live anew, that the bread his body, and the wine his blood.*

The word tells us that we should not drink the blood of animals, (sheep etc), that the life is in the blood. Jesus told his followers as they took the last supper to drink it and eat the bread.

The bread was his body, and the wine his blood to remember Him by.

At first to me this didn't seem right, but we see that God is talking about the animal's blood and not human blood, so we can remember Jesus this way. So when we look at the grain of wheat that falls to the earth it dies but lives anew to make more seeds.

When we take the wine, as Jesus's blood, we are that new seed of Jesus as we give our lives to God. We are the new life to proclaim the kingdom of God to others in the world, in our own streets, towns, and cities.

When we take these elements we are saying to the Lord God that we will follow Him and do what God asks us to do. This may be hard for us to take orders from the mighty God, and to walk and talk with him.

Revelations 1: 18.

That Jesus has the keys of Death and Hades (hell), So we know that Jesus is the keeper of the keys, and that we should walk and talk with him.
That Jesus is the way, the truth, and the life.
So we must go through Jesus into the heavens to the Father.
As Jesus is the key holder. as Revelations said in 1: 18.

Jesus has the keys of Death and Hades.
To be in lineament with God our Father, we know that Jesus was in lineament
with the Father.

Jesus is the head of the church so man must be the head of his house. The woman is under the man so all men must be in lineament with Jesus.

So we have God with Jesus, then man and then woman, so all three are in lineament under God. If we move out of lineament with God, then things go wrong and we fall away from God.

So we have God, then under God Jesus, then man is under Jesus, then woman under man.

So has the church watered down the word so we accept the word and not live the word? Has the church become weaker in its preaching? Have we moved out of lineament with God, that we are not walking and talking with our God.

All through the Bible we read that God is calling us to Himself but nothing is happening. We sit in our churches and hear that things are happening without results. We sing and some people will pray. We walk out of church until the next Sunday morning service and we're back again to do the same thing over again.

God is the A and the Z, the Alfa and Omega, the beginning and the end.

God wants us seven days a week to remember that He (God) created the world in six days. He created the world in six days, then He rested on the seventh.

God wants us to worship and pray to Him on Sundays, but also to remain in Him through the reading of his word every day.

One morning the man was in prayer giving thanks to the Trinity for all that they had done for us. And he started to wonder when Jesus was on the Cross. As they came to take Him down how did they take the nails out of His hands and feet for they would have been well nailed? Would they have pulled His hands over the heads of the nails or did they remove them?

121

The bible doesn't tell us how they took him down, only that they put a linen cloth around Him and put Him into the tomb. The word, (Bible) does not say a thing about any tools to remove the nails?

Psalm 105:17 Joseph had to wait for the word to come.

The Psalm tells us that Joseph whose feet they hurt with fetters was led in irons. *V19* until the time that his word came, the word of the Lord to purified him.

We then must wait upon the Lord till our word comes.

When the word comes, we have to be ready to move. God will not wait for us, we have to jump to it, otherwise we can miss the timing of our God, we have to be in rhythm with Him (God).

One evening as the man was in the prayer room he was alone praying to God. And he was kneeling and it was if the man was having steel armor placed on him bit by bit, his arms then his feet and legs. His whole body was getting covered. The man was getting worried about this and said to God, "what is happening?" God replied and said *"that He, God was placing His armor on him so it would protect him. God also said this would be able to repel any of the evil spirits that comes against him, and that he would stand strong against them".*

As the man went to stand up he could feel the armor upon on him. He recalls the story of King David when Saul put his armor on David, he was going against the Giant and he couldn't move, that's how he felt. God said *that all will be well, that he would know the authority that God had given him and the other three prayer partners.*

On one occasion the man and the prayer partners were asked to pray over this house. They were praying in the kitchen when he saw spirits outside the window looking in. He rebuked them and as the other prayer partners were moving to the upstairs bedrooms he also moved upstairs with them.

There was a toilet to the left and as he moved to the door he felt the movement of something passing him. Then moving into the bedroom where the others were he was at the end of the bed and as the prayers were going on he was pushed back hitting the wall. He got angry with the spirits and started to rebuke them casting them from the house in the name of Jesus. He had the power in Jesus's name as he cried out.

This was told to the owner and they asked him to continue to pray over the house daily to keep God's covering over the home.

The spirits knew they were there to cast them out. The man was not going to let the spirits push them around. He was going to stand his ground as God had given him the power. So when God gives you the power use it in His name.

When God opens people's eyes they see lots of things that God wants them to see. Many times the man and his prayer partners would be asked to pray over homes so they would come against the powers of darkness. One day they were praying for this home the people had just moved into. As they moved into the kitchen this small girl came up to them and was crying, she was a lost spirit. The man said to her that they were sorry but she would have to leave the house, she pleaded with him and was holding their hands. There is nothing we can do with wandering spirits, and the world is full of them.

Proverbs 2: 1-5.

My son, if you will take my words and hide my commandments, with you v2 so that you incline your ear to wisdom, applying your heart to understanding, v3 and if you cry after intelligence, and lift up your voice for understanding, v4 if you seek it as silver, and search for it as for hidden treasures, v5 then you will understand, the reverence of the Lord, and find the knowledge, of God.

So you can see that when God wants you to have the different gifts, take hold of them and do not let anyone take them away from you, because there are people that will try to, yes, even within the church.

Proverbs 4: 13,

Take fast hold of instruction. Do not let it go! Keep it, for it is your life! v14 Do not enter the path of the wicked! Do not go in the way of bad people! v15 Avoid it, Evil! Do not pass by it! Turn from it and pass away v16 for they do not sleep, except they have chosen evil, And their sleep is taken away, unless they cause some to fall. v17 for they eat the bread of wickedness and drink the wine of violence.

v18 But the path of the just is like the shining light that shines more and more
until the day is established.
v19The way of the wicked is like darkness, they do not know at what they stumble.
v20 My son, pay attention to my words, incline your ear to my sayings.
v21 Do not let them depart from your eyes! Keep them in the midst of your Heart!

God's word is so true that we must continue to read His word daily and to talk with Him. These scriptures that I have used are just a starting point, you must read on right through the Bible to understand it. The man must admit he reads it every day and he still does not understand it, but he knows that when he reads it God speaks to him.

As I am writing it, God is there telling me what I should be writing. God wants you to come to Him.

This is what God has just said to me.

So this is not me but God calling you to come.

Proverbs 5: 1,

My son, pay attention to my wisdom, bend your ear to my understanding.
v2 So you can heed discretion and so your lips can keep knowledge.

I would like to recall a time that I had a heart attack, I was in hospital and the nurse was prepping me for heart surgery.

As I was lying on the bed at around 7 pm I was talking to my wife at the time. I looked up and sitting on the curtain rail was a sparrow, I said to my wife look at the sparrow. I know I had peace about the operation the next day but this was very special. I knew that it was God, He was going to be with me through the operation. The day they moved me back into the ward after a number of days in intensive care, sitting on the window sill outside was YES the sparrow, I know that I know it was God making sure I was back.

124

Gate Twenty-Nine

When we read Proverbs it talks about sitting at the gates. When we go through life and different things come against us we need to sit at the gates of whatever it is. We must sit at the gate and wait for God. To seek His will in this matter, then the Holy Spirit will guide us through, and move us to the right gate. He will open it, and take us down the right path, if we do not wait then we could take the wrong Gate.

In *Exodus 32:27* Moses was instructing the followers of God to go from gate to gate to slay the people who had sinned. At the time the people were not in a walled city with gates.

So what gates was Moses talking about?

The gates of life?

The gates of sin?

or

The gates of disobedience?

In *Genesis 18*: Abraham was with God, and it was at the time of the destruction of Sodom and Gomorrah. Abraham asked God "will you destroy all the people or just the wrong doers?" Only Lots family were saved. I wonder if at the end of time it will be like Sodom?

When we read about Lazarus, he was at the gate of the rich man wanting food. They both died, Lazarus went up to Abraham, the rich man went down to Hades (Hell).

Now the rich man saw Lazarus up in Heaven and wanted water to cool his mouth. Abraham said one can't pass from one side to the other, as we go through the gates we must choose the best gates, the PEARLY or the HADES (HELL) gates.

So we must come to God and worship him with all, Yes all we have, as God said Come to ME.

Are you there yet?

Now after many years and many gates, in 2013 God opened my eye Gate to see and know what the birds were saying to him, (That God wanted His people closer to Him. Another gate opens).

God opens or closes or locks the gates, for its in His time He makes all things come to pass.

How do we come closer to God, through his word in prayer, in praise and through his whisper?

For its our way of opening the gate to spend time with God our creator and we get to know his Son, also the Holy Spirit in a wonderful way no matter where or when or time, we can connect with the Father, Son and Spirit.

We must listen very carefully to the voice of Jesus, learn to know the voice, the wrong voice will take us through the wrong gate.

The Spirit leads us to the Father, and the Father locks the gates when it's not His leading. We may think the grass is greener on the other side, and Satan will try and take us on a different path, or try and open the gate.

We must know the voice of God, the voice of the Son, and the voice of the Spirit, the gate of opening our ears to the right voice.

Jesus said to the people you hear but don't know, when we hear the shepherd we (the sheep) will go and follow through the right gate.

We have a true intimacy and fellowship with the Holy Spirit, to know His voice and to be joined together, to know the difference between His and the other voices we hear.

Psalm 23 God is with us always.

When we go through the gate of fire.

When we go through the gate of water.

When we go through the gate of death God is with us through all the gates of our lives. Jesus said He would never leave us or forsake us the Trinity wants us near to them, the closer we get the better it is for us.

The teaching gate

Jesus was asked where did He get his teaching from? He answered, from the one who sent Him (God his Father). Many in God's churches today have omitted the Holy Spirit in their lives, and it is just Father and Son. We must have the Trinity the three in one in us, the Father, Son and the Spirit, as it is the spirit that teaches us God's ways so we must go through the three gates.

Well the road is not an easy one, there is ups and downs but when we have God on our side there is no problem. God takes on the evil one that tries to take us away from God.

When we stay in God's word, we become strong to stand up against the enemy. God gives us the power and the know-how. God's protection is so strong and his love for us is so wonderful.

God will work in your life as He has in mine. He takes us through many gates, some are to protect us and many are to teach us. Many to guide us to the right path that God wants us to be on.

Just like chess, moving us to the next place to work for Him.

Matthew 16: 19 I shall give you the keys of the Kingdom of the Heavens, and whatever you would bind upon the Earth will already have been bound in the heavens and whatever you would loose upon the Earth will already have been loosed in the heavens.

Are you in darkness?

Are you in the wilderness?

Are you facing a giant?

Is life not going the right way for you? Then the only way for you is to seek the Lord God. For He is the only way, and the only one who can put things right for you.

God's word tells us that He God,

127

Is the WAY

He is the TRUTH

And He is the LIFE

He is the Master of us all, nothing, absolutely nothing is impossible for Him. God is the creator God and He loves us so much that He gave His one and only SON for us. *JOHN 3:16.*

A word of encouragement read in *LUKE 10:24.*

It says: for I say to you that many prophets and kings wanted to see what you are seeing but they did not see, and to hear what you are hearing but they did not hear.

Deuteronomy 5:20
And it was, when you heard the voice out of the midst of the darkness, while the mountain burned with fire, that you came near to me, all the heads of your tribes, and your elders 21. and you said, 'behold, the LORD our God has shown us His glory and His greatness and we have heard His voice out of the midst of the fire. We have seen this day that God does talk with man, and he lives. 22. Now therefore, why should we die? For this great fire will consume us if we hear the voice of the LORD our God any more, then we will die. 23. For who is there of all flesh, who has heard the voice of the Living God speaking out of the midst of the fire as we have, and lived? 24. Go near and hear all that the LORD our God will say and speak to us everything that the LORD our God will speak to you and we will hear it and do it.'

This reading is from the One New Man Bible

by William J. Morford.

Revealing

JEWISH ROOTS AND POWER

If you seek Him, He will be found by you, but if you forsake Him, He will cast you off forever.

This is where King David is Instructing Solomon his son.

Lightning Source UK Ltd.
Milton Keynes UK
UKHW021046060722
405457UK00008B/1604